A Commotion in Your Heart

Notes on Writing and Life

Barbara Shoup

Copyright © 2019 by Barbara Shoup

All rights reserved.

A Commotion in Your Heart: Notes on Writing and Life by Barbara Shoup

ISBN: 978-1-7324993-1-7

Book design by Andrea Boucher

Printed in the United States of America

This book is for my students, who have enriched my life immeasurably.

Also by Barbara Shoup:

Novels

An American Tune

Looking for Jack Kerouac

Everything You Want

Faithful Women

Vermeer's Daughter

Stranded in Harmony

Wish You Were Here

Night Watch

Nonfiction

Novel Ideas: Contemporary Authors Share the Creative Process

Story Matters

Contents

Introduction
The Underground Railroad 1

Why Write?
Standing on the Sidewalk 5
Driving at Night 6
A Commotion in Your Heart 9
Carrots 14
Misbelief 17

Debunking the Myths
Combustion 23
Piece of Cake 27
The New Girl 31
But That's How It Happened 32
What We Talk About When We Talk About Writing 37
Chasing the Muse 41

What They Said
Kurt Vonnegut's Blessing 44
Paul Klee's Sketchbook 46
Piero's Byzantine Hats 47
Hemingway's Iceberg 51
Captain Fiction's Assault 54
The Diary of Samuel Pepys 57
Muriel Sparks' Consolation 60
Edith Wharton's Grave 62

Fiction 101
Before and After   69
Up in Michigan   74
"We Was Girls Together"   78
The Hitler Dollhouse   83
"Y'all Had Enough Yardbird?"   87
Dr. Beat and the Archangels   94
Drawing Boxes   99
A Day in the Life   103

Jump
Take a Deep Breath   107
Then What?   111
When Do I Put in the Symbols?   118
Working (a Jigsaw)   120
Mind the Gap   127
The Revision Toolkit   130

The Writing Life
New York, New York   139
The Voices in My Head   148
(Maybe) Don't Quit Your Day Job   152
Three Ways to Look at Being Famous   157

Introduction

The Underground Railroad

FROM THE MOMENT I LEARNED TO READ, I read—anywhere, everywhere. Walking home from school, at the dinner table, in the car, in bed with a flashlight when I was supposed to be asleep. A book was the most amazing thing! Open one and a life completely unlike my own unfolded. I was alive in a place I'd never been.

I was maybe seven when I realized that books weren't magic. People wrote them, and those people were called authors. More than anything else in the whole world, I wanted to be one. So, I started writing stories in blue notebooks I bought at the dime store. I kept them in a secret place.

Around that same time, on a summer evening, I'd just had my bath, and I was in bed—drowsy, although it was still light. I could hear the voices of neighborhood kids still playing outside. And for some reason I will never understand, I was overwhelmed by the sudden, visceral knowledge that someday I would not *be*. It terrified me. I lay perfectly still for a long time, my heart beating wildly. One good thing, I told myself: Books live forever. Which meant, if I wrote books, I could live forever, sort of, too.

Then there was the problem of money: My family never had enough. There were so many things I wanted but couldn't have—nice clothes, a nice house, a room of my own. *Authors are rich*, I thought. *They must be!* So, when I became an author, I would be rich, too. All our problems would be solved, and we would be happy.

I wrote and wrote and wrote. I also began to pay attention to the wider world. As I did, I discovered that other people had problems, too. Every night, on the TV news, I watched white people scream and throw things at black children who were just trying to go to school. I knew this was hateful and wrong—and that the problem had started a long time ago, with slavery. In a leap of imagination, I decided to write about a girl my age escaping a plantation, traveling north by Underground Railroad. It would be more than a story, though. It would be a *whole book*.

I came home from school every day, closed my bedroom door behind me, and worked until I got my story told. It was forty pages long! I copied it on clean paper in my best handwriting, made a green construction paper cover, and wrote a title on it: *Slave Girl*. Then I took a deep breath and sent it off to a New York publisher whose address I'd found in a library book.

Then we got to the unit in social studies that explained that the Underground Railroad was not a subway train that ran from Atlanta to New York City.

I felt so humiliated. It made my stomach hurt to think about people in New York reading my book and laughing. *You are too stupid to be an author,* I told myself. *Quit now, before you make a bigger fool of yourself than you already have.*

And I did quit. For nearly twenty years.

Then, one day—when I was almost thirty, with a husband and two daughters I adored, and a teaching job I found exciting and fulfilling—I was hanging out with a group of my high-school students, listening to them talk about what they planned to do when they grew up. One of them turned to me and asked, "What about you?"

I laughed. "I am grown up. Remember? I'm your teacher."

He pressed me, as teenagers do. "But is that what you *want* to do?"

"I love my job," I said. "Teaching makes me happy." This was true.

"But did you always want to be a teacher?" he asked. "Is teaching the only thing you ever wanted to do?"

I'd buried my dream of writing so deep that his questions rattled me to the core. I couldn't just brush him off. Nor could I ignore the voice inside me saying, *You still want to be a writer. You never stopped wanting to be a writer.* I'd sworn to myself that I wouldn't be one of those adults who lied to kids or avoided hard questions. I couldn't lie or dissemble now. So, I said, as casually as I could manage, "Oh, once I wanted to be a writer."

"Wanted?" he asked. "You don't want it anymore?"

I shrugged. He kept looking at me. I knew the time had come.

"Lyfe so shorte, Crafte so harde to learne," Chaucer wrote. So true. Nearly 45 years after that conversation with my student, I'm still learning about writing. *A Commotion in Your Heart* shares what I've learned so far. If you long to be a writer, I hope this book will give you the courage to begin. If you're already a writer but need to be reminded that, though writing often seems impossible, it's not, I hope it will help you hold steady on the path.

Why Write?

Standing on the Sidewalk

A SUMMER EVENING. TWILIGHT. I'M IN THE car with my family—my parents in front; my brother, sisters, and me squashed into the back. As we round the corner to our block, I see a dozen or more kids in the Corrigans' front yard. They're facing each other in two rows, arms locked. All the kids on one side sing out, "Red Rover, Red Rover, send Jimmy right over!" Jimmy Corrigan bursts from one line and runs full-tilt toward the other, his teammates screaming, "Go, go, go, go, go!"

By the time I get out of the car and run across the street to play, Mrs. Corrigan is on the porch, calling her kids in for the night. The game disperses, the winners full of themselves for winning, the losers pretending they don't care, and I'm left standing on the sidewalk, invisible.

It took me a long time to realize why that moment—rounding the corner, seeing the neighborhood kids playing Red Rover—not only imprinted itself so indelibly on my mind, but carries with it such a rush of longing every time it surfaces: It was a snapshot of how childhood was supposed to be—that is, my *idea* of how childhood was supposed to be, based on books. There it was, right there in my own neighborhood—and all I'd managed was a glimpse of it through the car window.

One summer evening, years later, I stood just inside the doorway of a tiny town hall in northern Michigan, watching my husband dancing with our two daughters. The crowded dance floor, the townie band in the corner, the ladies selling baked goods—*my own family*. It was as if I was looking at them through the wrong end of a telescope. They seemed separate. Foreign. Unreachable. Writing now, I see them with the same mix of love, loneliness, and melancholy I felt that night.

I've had moments like this all my life. So has every other serious writer I know. We are the children standing on the sidewalk, watching other kids play; the teenagers and adults who gravitate to the edge of a party or sit quietly at the dinner table watching the little dramas playing out around us. We are here, but not here. We don't fit in the real world. Something in us is constantly watching, trying to figure things out. We write to create fictional worlds that help us understand the real world a little better. Paradoxically, those fictional worlds are made of bits and pieces of the real world. How could it be otherwise?

Driving at Night

"WRITING IS LIKE DRIVING AT NIGHT," THE novelist E.L. Doctorow wrote. "You can see only as far as the headlights. But you can make the whole trip that way." He was referring to the way ideas reveal just enough of themselves to keep you moving toward a finished story. But *becoming* a writer is like that, too. You start out in the dark, seeing only what's directly ahead of you, trusting that if you keep going and stay alert, the road beneath you will teach you what you need to know as you go.

I like this idea for a lot of reasons—not the least of which is that my first big epiphany about writing came while I was driving a vanload of sleeping teenagers back to Indiana after a wonderful but exhausting week of exploring New York City together. I felt utterly alone and weightless in the midnight darkness, the interstate an endless black ribbon beneath my wheels. My eyes were scratchy with fatigue, shocked again and again into opening fully each time the white line of the highway went wobbly and the van swerved ever so slightly toward the berm. But it was my turn to drive, and it didn't seem fair to wake the other chaperone and ask him to take his shift early.

Loud music helped, and rolling my window down to let in the cool night air. But it was a single thought that jolted me back into full consciousness—a cartoon moment, the proverbial light bulb switching on above my head. I remember nothing about the train of thought that brought me to the moment, just the idea itself—*sometimes there is no word*—and the suddenness with which it brought me awake to…well, everything.

By then, I'd gathered up the courage to try to write. But I couldn't understand how I could feel filled up with a story, sense its shape, see its places in my mind's eye, know its people—and then *not* be able to write it. I was baffled by the all-too-frequent experience of obsessively flipping through my thesaurus from one not-quite-right word to another, looking for the one I felt and knew but could not find. Until that moment in the dark van, it had not occurred to me that the word I was searching for might not exist.

The thought excited me. What if it *wasn't* my abysmal vocabulary, mediocre intelligence, or lack of training as a writer that kept me from being able to neatly match ideas and images with words? What if there was an unbridgeable gap between what it feels like to be human and the words available to a writer—*any* writer—to express it?

"Wake up!" I wanted to shout. "I just realized the most amazing thing!" But I didn't. And after that first impulse to share my amazing news, I found myself enjoying the long night drive, alone with my discovery of the paradox at the very center of writing fiction: Nothing we observe, feel, or know about our own human experience or the experience of others comes to us by way of words. And yet, words are all we have to make a story in which living, breathing characters move through worlds that seem as real to readers as their own back yard. No writer has ever had or will ever have all the words needed to re-create the world that was alive in their mind. Jane Austen had to come to terms with this. So did William Faulkner and Toni Morrison.

As I drove into the dawn, I realized something even weirder: Writing a story is not unlike translating a story into another language. A translator must be fluent in two languages and cultures, must try and fail until the gap between the story in its first language and its second language is as narrow as it can be—accepting that it is impossible for the second language to convey the story perfectly. Similarly, writers must be fluent in the language in which they are writing, master the craft of fiction, know the world of the story—accepting that words are a second language to the heart. Writing is all about finding and combining the words available to you, trying and failing until the story on the page is as close as it can be to the one inside you.

Flooded with relief, I thought, *I can do that!*

And I did—collecting moments of intuition along the way that deepened my understanding of what writing really is and how it works. Some of these came out of the blue—in solitary moments like the one I just described, or in the middle of writing a story. Others came during spirited conversations with other writers or while talking to students about what writers do and helping them struggle through their own stories.

Some writers just write. That's enough for them. But over time, I became as obsessed with the *process* of writing stories as I was with the stories themselves. Those moments of intuition never fail to excite me. It's tempting to say that they feel like pieces of a puzzle clicking into place—they *do* feel that way—but it's a puzzle that can never be solved. How can you expect to understand the way the human mind works when creating a story, when all you have is a human mind to understand it *with*?

It's impossible, of course. But writers are people who keep trying anyway.

A Commotion in Your Heart

I'D BE RICH IF I HAD A dollar for every time a would-be writer said to me, "But my life is so boring, I have nothing to write about." Everyone's life is interesting; everyone has a story to tell. Your own material—your "stuff"—is, simply, everything in your life, large and small, that has ground the lens through which you see the world.

This world view is pretty much set by the end of your adolescence, and within it lay the rich, unanswerable questions you will spend your whole life exploring through stories. As you grow older, changes in yourself and in the world complicate and deepen those questions. You come to understand your present and past life experiences in new and different ways. But the questions you asked when you were young never change…and are never answered.

Camus said, "A man's work is nothing but a long journey through the detours of art to the two or three simple and great images which first gained access to his heart."

Here are mine.

I'm four years old, waiting at the back door for my father to come home from work. My heart lifts when I see him turn the corner from the bus stop and start down the alley: young, handsome, smiling. Mine.

This was before we were a family with four stair-stepped children. Before there was never enough money to pay the bills and buy what we needed to live comfortably. Before we moved to a cramped pre-fab house in the suburbs, where life became more than my dad could handle, and he began drinking to get through the day. By the time I was in high school, there was little left of the father I'd adored as a little girl. I grieved for him as if he had died, grieved for the family we might have been.

Why does it have to be this way?

I write about families and how they shape us, still trying to understand what happened to my own.

I'm maybe nine, and I can't stop looking at a china plate my mother had promised would be mine someday. It is the most beautiful thing I've ever seen: delicately made, rectangular, covered with pink and blue cornflowers, edged in gold.

When or how the plate was broken, I don't remember. Just that terrible sense of something that can't be undone—and feeling cheated and angry, as if something had been stolen from me. One beautiful thing, the only beautiful thing in our house, and now it was gone. Years later, in the Mauritshuis Museum in Holland, I stood riveted before the painting "View of Delft" by Johannes Vermeer. I wanted to walk into the painting—to live there forever. I felt the same intense pleasure I'd felt looking at that china plate mixed with the deep sense of loss I felt when it was broken.

Why can't everything we cherish last?

I write to capture things I've lost or know I'll lose—people, paintings, objects, places, a butterfly wing—as a way of owning them. Forever.

I'm sixteen, flung across my bed, miserable, dateless on prom night, certain that nobody will ever love me. Why would they? I will always, always be alone.

I was a disaster as a teenager. Flat-chested and so skinny I wore two pair of knee-socks to make my legs seem less twig-like. My dishwater-blond hair was thin and straight and always looked horrible, even though I slept on torturous prickly rollers every night. I was too loud and, in my view, only passably smart—certainly not smart enough to take journalism and hang out with the kids on the school newspaper, which was the one place I felt like I might belong. Secretly, more than anything, I wanted to be a writer. *Nobody* knew this about me, and I'd never have admitted it, even in the unlikely event that someone guessed.

What is wrong with me? Will I ever belong?

I write to try to understand who I was then, why I was so miserable—and how hard it is at any age to be your true self and find your place in the world.

And this—not an image or a memory, but just as powerful—something fundamental I came to understand about my mother and myself:

A war bride's first child
Even before breath
I heard her crying

My material—family relationships, a yearning for beauty and the heartbreak of loss, the intensity of adolescence—has been present in varying degrees in everything I've written for more than forty years. I'm never bored by it. And I'm nowhere near knowing everything it has to teach me about who I am and what it means to be alive.

Your material is right there inside you, too—like the shifting shapes in a kaleidoscope, just waiting to fall into one of an infinite number of designs. To find it, let your memory range back to the defining moments in your life. Look intensely at these moments. Pay attention to what floats up again and again, the way disparate experiences combine themselves. Look for patterns. Notice single moments, crystal clear in your memory, resonating down through time.

Richard Ford said, "Find what causes a commotion in your heart. Find a way to write about that."

Sometimes students say, "But that stuff is so sad." If I think they're tough enough, I share a favorite Hemingway quote of mine: "Madame, all stories, if continued far enough, end in death, and he is no true-storyteller who would keep that from you." If I don't think they're ready for that yet, I remind them that we don't live forever, and that although all art flows from that sad fact, it doesn't mean *life itself* is sad.

It also doesn't mean that all good stories are sad. In fact, some of the stories I love best are hilarious. The indignant narrator in Eudora Welty's "Why I Live at the P.O." makes me laugh out loud every time I read the story—but I also sense the pain caused by the way her family indulges her selfish sister. And Tim O'Brien's double-edged war stories make me laugh and cry at the same time.

Besides, the range of human emotions is vast, their complexity infinite. Who hasn't gotten the giggles at a sad or somber event? Who hasn't felt sadness wash over them in the midst of a happy moment, if for no other reason than knowing it will end?

In case you're wondering, discovering and working with your material doesn't mean your stories will be autobiographical. Some writers do spend their whole careers telling and retelling the stories of their own lives, telescoping events, reordering them, shifting the focus, changing the point of view, adding fictional elements. More often, though, stories grow from kernels of experience, picking up bits and pieces of the world along the way. My novel, *Vermeer's Daughter*, is set in 17th century Holland, but at its heart is my longing to be close to my father.

Think of standing in a dressing room with opposite mirrors—how, when you look at yourself at the mirror in front of you, your image repeats itself in the mirror behind you into infinity. That's how many stories you have within you.

Carrots

ONCE, DRIVING BACK HOME TO INDIANA AFTER a solitary week of writing in northern Michigan, an open semi filled with carrots passed me on the road. The carrots were piled high in the bed, sticking through the slats on the side—thousands of them, disappearing into the distance as the truck pulled away.

I was alone. It was a long trip. I couldn't stop thinking about the carrots. How many were there in the truck? Where did they come from? Where were they going? How did farmers know how many carrots to plant each spring? How did they know what to do with them when—*wait*, I thought. Do carrots get ripe? What do you call a *finished* carrot? How does a restaurant or grocery store know how many carrots to order? How do carrots *work*?

The logistics of carrots quickly overwhelmed me, as logistics often do. Then came an existential question: If I could understand the logistics of carrots, would I, at long last, understand how the world worked?

When I shared this thought with my very sensible husband, S., he looked at me like I was insane. But the idea kept its hold on me. Over the next few weeks, I told the carrot story to several other people. Those who navigated the world with ease responded exactly as S. had, while those who found the world confounding knew exactly what I meant. Not surprisingly, that latter group was made up almost entirely of fellow writers. It took more than twenty years, but that truckload of carrots finally made its way into a book—the one you're reading now—just as I knew, eventually, it would.

Sometimes, quirky details seem to be gifts from the cosmos, offered just when you need them. That happened to me during another solo retreat to Michigan. One afternoon, walking along the beach at Sleeping Bear Dunes, I saw in the distance a young man lugging big rocks from the water to the shore. As I grew closer, I realized he was using the rocks to spell something in the sand.

"What...?" I asked, when I reached him.

"'Will you marry me,'" he answered. He pointed to a place on a bluff above and said he planned to take his girlfriend there that evening.

I was near the end of writing *An American Tune*, a novel about a woman whose life begins to unravel when an unexpected encounter with the man she loved in college threatens to reveal a secret she's kept from her family. Parts of the book are set on the beach where I was walking that day, and I immediately recognized the detail of the young man spelling out his proposal as the gift that it was. Later that day, I sat down at my desk and wrote:

Early last summer, she had passed a young man, nineteen or twenty, wrapping a dozen or so good-sized stones at a time into a blanket, then dragging it down the beach a ways to dump them on the sand. She had thought he was making one of the sculptures that had been mysteriously appearing on the beach in the last year or so, but on her way back she saw that he had lined the stones in vertical groups and was in the process of forming each group into a letter.

She stopped, curious, and asked, "What in the world are you spelling?"

He grinned. "Will you marry me?" He waved his arm toward the southernmost letter "See?"

Nora had thought it was an "M," facing the water, but now saw that it was a "W" facing the lookout point at the top of the steep dune, high above them. Next to it, "I-L-L. Then Y-O-U M-A-R."

"How long have you been here?" she asked.

"Couple of hours," he said. "I still have to get the stones for the rest of the letters, so I figure it'll take me at least another two. Man, I'll tell you what. I'm bringing my girlfriend up here this evening. She better say yes!"

But he knew she would, Nora could tell, and it had made her feel weepy to think of the girl's first look at the words on the beach below, how she would turn to him and in his face see that they were meant for her.

"Take a picture to show your grandchildren," she had said to him, lightly as she could, and walked away, thinking that he couldn't imagine how quickly the time would pass, how the grandfather he'd become would still be, in part, the kid he was now: tanned, strong, crazy in love.

All of this is to say, pay attention!

The whole world is your material. The bits and pieces of it you need to make your stories come alive are everywhere. Jot them down in a notebook, snap photos, or trust your brain to spit out the perfect detail when you need it. Use those details just as they are, or as a springboard for something imagined. Ask, *What if?* Combine them in unlikely ways. Play them out in your writer's mind.

Learn to see—to *really see*—the world you live in. Trust that it has in it every single thing you will ever need.

Misbelief

DEPRESSION WAS A WORD I NEVER HEARD growing up in my working-class, post-war neighborhood. Someone might be sad, downhearted, or grief-stricken, or—and this was always whispered—might have had a nervous breakdown. This meant that that the person had been so sad, downhearted, or grief-stricken that they went crazy. Sometimes they even had to be locked up in a mental institution. As far as I know, this didn't happen to anyone I knew as a child. But, eavesdropping, I heard people use the phrase plenty of times. There were rumors of nervous breakdowns, worries that this person or that might be having one. Sometimes people said, "I swear, I'm about to have a nervous breakdown," but they were joking. Some probably feared it was true but would never have said so or asked for help.

What would a nervous breakdown look like? I wondered. How would it feel?

I was a sad child, and I became sadder as I grew into adolescence—so sad that I began to believe it was just a matter of time before *I* had a nervous breakdown. To be honest, it kind of thrilled me. The drama! The idea that my parents would finally look at me—*really* look at me—and see that they needed to do something to make me feel better!

In my mid-twenties, in the aftermath of a close friends imprisonment, I thought I might actually be having one. Grief pinned me down. Thoughts of how I'd failed my friend—how I'd failed everyone, not least of all myself—looped through my mind with no relief. Nothing made me feel better. All I wanted to do was sleep. I was incapable of joy. I did only what I absolutely had to do in a state of lethargy so profound I felt drugged.

There was no drama. It wasn't thrilling. I was scared. Alarmed, S. finally convinced me to "talk to someone."

I doubt I even knew the word *therapist* then. Probably I looked up "mental health" in the *Yellow Pages*. In any case, I got lucky. I found a good therapist—a scruffy guy, probably in his early thirties. He listened to my story about my friend. He asked me questions that drew out the fact that I'd been sad for most of my life—and that, while I'd never want to do what my friend did, I envied the passion that drove her to it. I admitted that I was bored staying at home with my children; I had a teaching degree but I wasn't using it. I had chosen these things, but they made me feel invisible.

"You're depressed," he said, when I was through. "You're not like the women who want nothing more than a family life. It's OK to be different, to want more."

S. had been saying more or less the same thing to me that the therapist said, but now I *heard* it. A weight lifted from me. I got a job working at a high school, as part of a special program that used alternative teaching methods, where I found a deeply satisfying life of my own.

I'm cured! I thought.

But I continued to experience cycles of what I now know was depression—"the dark treadmill," as I came to think of it. Sometimes it was tied to events, sometimes it came on for no reason I could see. Gradually, it would fade away. Once, the evening light drew me to the front window in our dining room, which looks out on the park across the street. The heavy sky was a troubled blue-gray, but the sun hidden behind made it shimmer. Then, a shaft of light fell upon the park, illuminating a swath of budding trees. The silver slide, the swings' silver chains, gleamed. The blue trashcans turned translucent. And, just like that, the darkness in me dissolved. The relief of it brought me to tears.

Despite those numerous bouts with depression, despite my dawning understanding that depression was a fairly common trait among creative people, I hadn't returned to therapy. *You know what's wrong with you*, I told myself. *You're different. It's OK to be different, but difficult. Deal with it.* But when S. had a near-fatal motorcycle accident—the shock of which was complicated by my failure to sell a second novel (and, of course, all the childhood stuff)—I found myself in trouble again. So, I opened the *Yellow Pages*. The therapist I'd seen before was no longer listed, so I randomly picked another one.

My good luck in picking therapists held. I loved Dr. J., an attractive woman in her sixties with lovely white hair and a kind, intelligent face. I always felt better in her presence. We talked; it helped. At her suggestion, I tried a new drug called Prozac. It helped, too. "Depression is an illness," Dr. J said. "If you had high blood pressure, you'd treat it. There's no reason not to treat depression, too."

What really made the difference in how I saw the world and myself in it was a book she lent me, called *Do It Yourself Happiness* by Lee Schnebly. The book featured a test to help readers identify the beliefs formed by childhood experiences that were creating problems in their adult lives. While this test revealed numerous insights into what I believed and why, what really blew me away was the part that asked readers to distill happy and unhappy childhood memories into single sentences that stated the belief each experience had formed.

In a happy memory, I'm in the children's section of the public library—a dim, cozy basement room lined with shelves of books. Entering, I breathe in the words, tingle with anticipation. What books will I carry home in my bicycle basket today? But I don't choose right away. I pull this book and that one from the shelves: new ones, old favorites, placing those I'm considering on the low bench where I'll sit to make my final decision. All this takes a long time because I never want to leave. It's so quiet here. Warm in the winter, cool in the summer. Watery light seeping down from the high windows. Then the pleasure of taking the books I've chosen to the checkout desk, where the librarian smiles at me approvingly and stamps each book and my pink library card with the due date.

I am happy in a dim, cozy room surrounded by books.

And I am. When I enter a library, that feeling of being at my childhood library never fails to rush back to into me. I want to stay there forever.

In an unhappy memory, my mom tells me to go to my grandma's house across the tracks to borrow twenty dollars. I want to ride my bike. She says no. I ride it anyway—and on the way home, I lose the twenty-dollar bill. Panicked, I backtrack. But I can't find it. I'm near tears, consumed with guilt, and terrified to tell my mom because I know how much she hates to ask for help in any way—especially when it involves money. Things must be really bad if she asked my grandma for twenty dollars, and now I've lost it. I know my mom won't ask again; what will we *do*?

Money is valuable and when it is lost it cannot be replaced.

I'm not rich now, but I lead a comfortable life. There's nothing I need or want that I can't figure out a way to have. Yet the smallest money gaffe—buying a pair of shoes that I have to abandon because they don't fit right, or an expensive dress that I don't end up liking so much after all—catapults me back into my seven-year-old self, overwhelmed by anxiety.

As it turned out, I had a long list of beliefs born of very specific moments in my childhood and adolescence. Whether formed from happy or unhappy experiences, each one subconsciously affected decisions I'd made and conclusions I'd drawn in my adult life. So, I set out to identify which of those beliefs were valid in my life now and which ones weren't.

The happy ones were still valid. Most of the ones born of unhappiness, however, no longer applied. But it wasn't as simple as deciding not to believe those things anymore. These early misbeliefs were shot into my psyche like an arrow. They were rooted there. Even today, they make me feel as I did in the unhappy moments that formed them, and they dictate my first impulse when making any decision that relates to them. I haven't learned to unbelieve them. I'm not sure it's possible. But I've learned to recognize those faulty beliefs for what they are and do my best not to allow them to influence how I live.

Do It Yourself Happiness made me curious about myself. The "bad Barb" loop of guilt and regret became less compelling than the pleasure of sorting out how these small and large moments had made me who I am. The book made me curious about other people, too. What formed them? What particular experiences created beliefs that were interfering in their ability to be happy? The world seemed completely different.

So did writing fiction. Strong characters are like real people, I realized—a hot mess of beliefs and misbeliefs formed as children that bring them to the moment a story begins. Plots hinge on misbeliefs, moving a character through a set of scenes that might bring insights that change the course of her life—or pitch her into a downward spiral.

Good therapy, books, and conversations that ask questions and offer insight about who you are, are a lot like good literary critique. They help you see and narrow the gap between the person you are inside and the one you present to the world. Therapy is revising *yourself*. It's about getting better and better. At the same time, it's about accepting that you'll always fall short of who you wanted to be but keeping on anyway.

Just like writing a story.

Debunking the Myths

Combustion

WHEN I TAUGHT CREATIVE WRITING TO HIGH-SCHOOL students, I required them to keep a journal, which I read each grading period and responded to with notes in the margins. The journal could be personal, or not—it was up to them. Most were personal. Their thoughts and memories and my responses to them became a kind of dialogue that helped me know my students better and guide each of them toward their best material.

For many, their material had to do with divorce. They grieved over their lost families, resented being used as pawns in their parents' arguments, were mortified when their parents fell in love with new people and acted like teenagers themselves, and envied the children of their parents' second families.

"We'll always love you. That will never change," their parents said.

When they remarried, they said, "Now four people love you."

Or as one student's mother, who'd struggled financially since her divorce said about her impending remarriage, "Things will be so much better. We can start over."

"*You* can start over," my student responded. "My parents will always be divorced."

Her words sliced through me. They still do. As do the words of another student, who described her father's constant criticism of her mother. "It hurts me so much," she wrote. "He doesn't know me well enough to know how much I'm like her."

Divorcing Baby Boomers remembered having a life before they met and married their exes, which made it easier to imagine a life for themselves and their children after the split. But, happy or unhappy, family was the only thing their children knew. The home they shared, the rhythm of daily life, the holiday traditions—even the arguments. They were all too often devastated when that life collapsed around them. Writing helped them ease the pain.

Reading my students' journals not only broke my heart, it made me realize that I was seeing something new in the universe. When I was in high school during the early 1960s, I knew one person with divorced parents. Now it was the late 1980s, and Baby Boomers' marriages were collapsing in unprecedented numbers. Because their own childhood families were still intact, nothing had prepared these Boomers to grasp the depth of their children's sorrow, or to recognize that some part of them would grieve the loss of their families forever.

How our families shape us, for better or worse—that's my material. So, even though I was happily married myself, I knew divorce was something I wanted—no, *needed*—to write about.

Debunking the Myths

I wasn't an Elvis fan as a teenager, but when a former student returned from Graceland and said it was a piece of Americana that shouldn't be missed, I talked a friend into a road trip to Memphis for the anniversary of Elvis's death. First on tap: a tour of the "mansion"—really just a big two-story colonial house on a busy commercial avenue. Our guide, a reverent college girl, showed us the dining room, its long table set with Priscilla's wedding china, and the living room, all white except for Elvis's gold piano. We saw the blue-and-yellow television room, with its whole wall of TVs, pull-down movie screen, jukebox, and soda fountain, where, in the early days, Elvis played soda jerk for his friends. There was the jungle room, with its dark paneling, brown wicker furniture, and shag carpet as green as grass; the pool room, its walls and ceilings covered by shirred fabric patterned in reds and blues—everything picked out by Elvis himself on a midnight trip to a furniture store.

Released into the intense August heat, we passed the swimming pool, its turquoise water sparkling in the sun, and then the meditation garden, a grotto-like space where Elvis was buried. Tributes littered the grave: plastic guitars wound round with roses, at least a dozen teddy bears, a pair of blue suede shoes. We ate cheeseburgers at the Heartbreak Hotel across the street and checked out the souvenir shop next door. There, we found everything from Elvis-style aviator sunglasses to Love Me Tender Shampoo.

That night, the city of Memphis closed the street in front of Graceland to accommodate the thousands of people who gathered to remember Elvis on the anniversary of his death. Loudspeakers blared Elvis ballads and gospel songs as a never-ending line of fans carrying candles wound their way up the path toward the grave—a fair number of them sobbing. Men, women, children; people on crutches and in wheelchairs; people speaking English, Spanish, French, and who knew what else.

"It's *wild*," my former student had said. She was right. Elvis's clothes, his cars, his airplane with solid gold seatbelts. The middle-aged ladies with ratted hair and caked-on makeup decked out in their Elvis fan club T-shirts, carrying Elvis tote bags. But there was something tender, too—as if Elvis held within him the youth they'd lost, the lives they'd dreamed of having when they were young.

How much he mattered to them hurt my heart.

At the time, I'd been thinking about my own youth and how quickly it had passed—and also about how so many people in my generation seemed to be having a really hard time admitting we were getting older. Music was in the mix—how a song could take you back to a moment of your life in such a visceral way, it seemed as if you were living it again. A few years later, my older daughter started dating a roadie. I was fascinated by the stories he told her about working for the rock 'n' roll greats. *A roadie would make a good character*, I thought—a divorced dad who never grew up.

All these things seemed connected, but I didn't have a *story*.

Then one of my students wrote in his journal about a friend who'd run away, and some kind of combustion occurred in my mind. *I knew.* The kid left behind was the main character. His parents were divorced. His dad was a roadie, his mom was a music teacher. They still loved each other, they always would, but they'd changed—or maybe it was that his dad *hadn't* changed, but his mom had grown up. In any case, this kid—Jackson was his name; I suddenly knew that, too—still grieved for the way things had been before his parents split. And now his best friend had taken off without a word, left him to navigate their senior year in high school all alone. Eventually, they'd end up at Graceland. It was as if all the ideas and images floating around in my head got into a car and hit the road. They knew where they were going. All I had to do was follow them.

Not that it was easy. They took a wrong turn now and then. There were breakdowns along the way that made me think we'd never get there. They got stuck sometimes. "What if this?" I'd ask them. "What if that?" Eventually, Jackson's journey to the next phase of his life became my first young adult novel, *Wish You Were Here*.

Sometimes people act like there's some elusive formula guaranteed to make a story gather and evolve. There isn't. That's a myth. There are, however, four elements that, one way or another, always come into play:

- **Your material:** The questions about your life you'll never be able to answer
- **The real world:** Countless details just waiting for a story
- **Combustion:** A kind of magic in your head that ignites a set of ideas and images and sets them moving into a story
- **Imagination:** Asking, *What if?* to keep things going until the end

Piece of Cake

BROWSING IN A BOOKSTORE ONE DAY, I came upon Gabriele Lusser Rico's *Writing the Natural Way: Using Right-Brain Techniques to*

Release Your Expressive Powers. The book was friendly inside, with lots of white space dotted with quotes about writing. There were these weird circles with words in them, with arrows pointing to other circles with words in them. They looped and meandered, sometimes taking up a whole page, sometimes whole facing pages. The book, which was based on recent brain research, offered a new way to think about and to teach writing.

Reading *Writing the Natural Way*, discovering how the whole brain works in the writing process and not just some mythical creative part of it, I felt a door opening to a world I'd felt unworthy of entering since childhood.

Until then, I hadn't really understood what *creative* meant. I hadn't even fully understood it was a process. I still thought the only problem was "translating" the stories inside you into words. Now I saw that the story itself was like quicksilver, constantly changing, difficult to contain. You had to trick it out of your brain onto the page. The book gave me a new and better way to talk to students about their writing and how to make it better. It *did* make their writing better, which made all of us happy. It made my writing better, too.

The brain research that provided the basis of Lusser Rico's book, published in 1983, is outdated now. But the essential message for writers hasn't changed: No single part of your brain is in charge of imagination or creativity. A good story is imagined and created through a series of wildly different tasks that your brain is cleverly designed to undertake.

For me, *Writing the Natural Way*'s simplified explanation of left- and right-brain functions remains a useful metaphor to help writers see how the whole head works to help or hinder the creative process. Think of the left side of your brain is like a computer. It defines and classifies the world you inhabit, holding everything you need to know and remember to live in it—from tying your shoes to solving a quadratic equation. It recognizes the symbols of the alphabet and knows how those symbols combine to make words. It remembers names, dates, and the definition of a sonnet.

The "computer brain" is analytical. It evaluates factual material rationally—that is, by standards that make sense, based on what people have in common. It processes information sequentially, one step at a time: one, two, three, four, five. But if six is missing, it shorts out and can't get to seven. This part of your brain is absolutely literal. For example, one time my five-year-old nephew said, "Piece of cake!" after his mom thanked him for solving a little problem. "Piece of cake?" his two-year-old brother said. "I want cake, too!" His mom tried to explain that there was no cake—that "piece of cake" just meant something was easy. "But I *want* cake," the two-year old wailed. He was stuck in his little left brain and couldn't be comforted.

Your left brain stores all the words you know, along with your mastery of grammar, sentence structure, and mechanics. Conscious and critical, this part of your brain is necessary to create a finished, polished piece of work. It's designed to analyze, edit, reshape, refine, and revise.

In contrast, the right side of your brain is like a slushie machine, constantly churning emotion, intuition, and memory, combining, connecting, and patterning them as it tries to make sense of the world. It makes and understands metaphor and idiom—for example, decoding the phrase "piece of cake" to "hey, no problem." It ranges wide and deep through your subconscious, making its own logic based on association.

It thinks in pictures, not words.

It's spatial, allowing you to sense the shape of a story.

It loves the unknown, the ambiguous, the paradoxical.

This part of your brain solves problems holistically, processing all kinds of information simultaneously and making great leaps of insight that are impossible for the step-by-step left brain. When you're cleaning out your sock drawer or driving around or dancing and—bingo!—the answer to what happened between character A and character B that made them hate each other pops into your mind as if from nowhere, it's this constantly ranging, exploring, considering part of your brain at work.

It's where ideas come from, where imagination resides. It brings focus and meaning to the clutter inside your head. Most important of all, this part of the brain gives your writing a voice, makes it uniquely your own.

For fun, Google "Left/right brain test" and take one of the many available to see where you fall on the scale. Don't agonize as you answer each question; go with your first, intuitive response. These tests don't prove that you have the stuff to be a writer—or that you don't. Your score will simply be a piece of information that might help you understand why some aspects of writing are easy for you and others are more difficult. For example, people who score higher on right-brain functions often have lots of ideas, a strong voice, and a knack for making interesting connections, but their stories may lack structure and coherence. In contrast, those who score higher on left-brain functions often write stories that are beautifully constructed but without the voice and detail to make them come alive. If you score somewhere in the middle, your brain is predetermined toward balance—although you might have to unlearn writing rules you learned in English class to take advantage of that. Fiction writers, especially novelists, tend to fall a little to the left of middle. This helps explain their knack for organization and logic in their work. Poets tend to fall to the far right—reflecting the role of patterning, imagery, rhythm, and association in theirs.

Ultimately, where you fall on the scale doesn't really matter. The brain is infinitely adaptable. Just as you might go to the gym and engage in a set of exercises designed to develop your biceps or quads, you can develop and fine-tune the traits your creative process demands.

The New Girl

A NEW GIRL, K., JOINED MY SIXTH-GRADE class mid-term. She was a writer—a very talented writer, according to our teacher. I was so jealous that I couldn't even bring myself to speak to her. I felt displaced, even though my teacher had no idea I wanted to be a writer. *Slave Girl*, the failed novel I'd written in fifth grade, had put an end to my dreams—and that was that.

The low point of the year was being cast in a play that K. wrote for our class. The script called for me to scream, but I couldn't manage to do it convincingly. "I know you can scream," the teacher said, in rehearsal. "I hear you on the playground." I was mortified.

K.'s writing accomplishments dogged me all through high school. The truth is, she was a nice girl, not at all stuck up. Looking back, I think we might have been friends. Becoming friends with her might have even given me the courage to take up writing again. But I was such a wreck as an adolescent, so certain I was completely without talent, that I'd have been embarrassed to make any kind of overture for fear of rejection.

K. didn't become a writer. I did. I don't take any satisfaction from this. I don't even know if she *wanted* to be a writer as an adult. Mainly, I'm bemused. K. *was* talented based on the standards by which most teachers recognize talent—a love of words, an impulse toward creative expression, an inborn knack for language that makes it easy to get a first draft on the page. But the most important talent K. had was belief in herself. She wanted to write, and she wrote.

Considering talent, it helps to imagine two runners: one with an inborn gift for going fast, the other who is only determined and well-disciplined. If the gifted runner trains seriously and is in great physical and mental shape, he'll beat the other runner every time. But if he parties too much, if he lacks the discipline to train regularly, he sets himself up to be beaten by the runner with less talent but more grit. The same is true of writers.

But That's How It Happened

RECENTLY, A WOMAN CALLED ME AT THE Indiana Writers Center to ask for advice about publishing a novel she'd written. It was based on the true story of a British ancestor who came to America in the 1800s. "He was related to King George," she said. "He knew

Queen Victoria!"

The woman's ancestor sailed to New Orleans with one hundred men and thirty wagons—horses and all, then traveled on to St. Louis. There, they outfitted the wagons with supplies, including small gifts for the Indians they'd heard so much about, before heading into the wilderness. According to a librarian, a dear friend of the caller, the book was "worth millions." Without a doubt, it would be made into a movie.

"So, I need you to find me an agent," the woman concluded. "My friend said I need to get this book on the market right away."

I took a deep breath. We get this kind of call a lot: people convinced they've just written a best-selling novel. I feel for them. It's not easy to write a novel—even a bad one. I do my best to be honest, helpful, and kind in my response. But few want to hear the truth about publishing, and most are unable or unwilling to learn what they need to know about writing fiction to write a publishable novel—not to mention coming to terms with the fact that even if they write a fabulous book, the odds of it earning millions are virtually nil.

Sure enough, this woman got huffy when I suggested she'd be wise to reconsider her expectations about money. She didn't want to hear that I couldn't provide an agent—or that even if I could, and even if the agent sold the book immediately, it would take a year, probably more, to get it into print. I wished her luck and said goodbye.

Not everyone's like that, though. Teaching at a writers' conference at Indiana University, I met another woman who'd attempted to novelize her family history. Her novel began with the family leaving Ireland for political reasons and coming to America. It went on, fact after fact, to present time. This book was deathly boring, but I was struck by one small detail: One day, not long after arriving in New Orleans and joining a fellow settler's blacksmith business, the woman's great-grandfather was left to mind the shop. An escaped slave entered and begged him to cut off his shackles. The woman's great-grandfather did so—after which time the family was ostracized to such an extent that they had to leave town.

"There's your novel!" I said. "The family flees to the land of the free, only to find out that not *everyone* is free. Tell that story and consider the book you've already written a family history." She did. She traveled to New Orleans to research the setting and wrote a wonderful young adult novel called *Simon*. Nearly eighty years old at the time, she self-published the book, and spent many happy days as a visiting author, sharing her stories with schoolchildren.

Another way to transform fact to fiction is to consider opposites. When S. had a near-fatal motorcycle accident many years ago, people said, "Oh, my God! That must have been horrible." I'd reply, "Well, yeah, it was." Then I'd try to explain that it wasn't *only* horrible. It was also sort of amazing. Wonderful things happened because of that crash. I learned that I was stronger than I'd imagined; friends brought us meals every night for weeks; and my husband and I grew closer than we'd ever been. Great material, you'd think. But the accident itself—while dramatic—didn't address any of my personal, unanswerable questions or even change my life in any fundamental way.

That got me thinking: What if a whole different kind of a dramatic event had happened? Something about which people would say, "Oh, my God. How fabulous! You're so lucky!"—And I'd feel at a loss to explain that this lucky thing had come with a set of tricky problems to solve, unanswerable questions to ponder.

Like winning a fifty million dollar lottery. My novel *Everything You Want* explores that possibility through a set of characters very much like my own family members. Flipping the experience of the motorcycle accident, delving deeply into something completely opposite, brought new understanding of the experience my family had shared.

In *Stranded in Harmony*, I attempted to come to terms with a friend's criminal act. I created characters based on the people involved in what actually happened, tried to feel the experience as those people had felt it, and to recreate their feelings in the story. But no matter how I tried, I couldn't make it work. *Finally*, the novel came together when, desperate, I left the literal truth and its long story behind and imagined an incident that had set the character's downfall in motion. I didn't even realize at the time that this imagined incident, related in less than a page, was truer, closer to the bone, and more devastating both to me and to the reader than any factual account could have been.

There's a lot of confusion among beginning writers about the relationship between fact and fiction. These writers are often wedded to the facts—and believe they're obligated to use every single one they know. Working with a true story, they think all they have to do to turn fact into fiction is tell it in the third person and change the names of the people involved. They don't understand that the particular set of facts they know constructs just one version of the event, and they miss the many other ways the story might be told. And they fail to grasp that life is stranger than fiction. Random things happen in life, but in fiction, each thing happens for a reason. If a fact or a scene doesn't serve a story, you leave it out. The same goes for people. If the real story had three sisters, but only two were significantly involved, that third sister no longer exists.

"But that's how it happened!" is how beginning writers often respond to a critic who suggests that something in a story doesn't work or doesn't belong. Conversely, seasoned writers often observe, "You'd never get away with that in a novel!" about unlikely real-life events.

Most of us are raised with a sense of moral obligation to "stick to the facts." We make decisions based on facts, argue our opinions based on facts, develop our judgments about people based on facts. Anything less is lying…and lying is bad. But all good fiction writers understand that nobody knows *all* the facts that come into play as real-life situations evolve. They understand that they might not even know what the facts they *do* know mean.

"I never read fiction," people sometimes say when they find out I'm a novelist. "I only read books that tell the truth." This makes me want to laugh. Don't they realize that nonfiction writers consider all the facts they've uncovered and choose the ones that help them shape the particular kind of story they want to write? If you read twelve books about a person, place, event, or period of time, each book will tell a different story—sometimes only slightly different, but sometimes wildly different. All are true stories, but none is the *only* true story that could be told.

Fiction tells its own kind of truth. The fiction writer's only agenda is to shape and tell a story in which an accumulation of facts—true and invented—reveals the human consequences of decisions and events. Good fiction makes the reader live in a story and come out of it with a greater understanding of real life.

What We Talk About When We Talk About Writing

MY WRITER FRIEND M. L. AND I read dozens of books about writing, searching for the perfect text to use in our classrooms. We found some really good ones, but no single book offered all three of the things we knew our students needed most: insight into the creative process, practical understanding of craft, and a hearty dose of inspiration. So, we decided to write that book: *Novel Ideas*. Then we wrote another one: *Story Matters*.

While completing our research for both of these books, we traveled coast to coast, interviewing writers about the way they worked—from Grace Paley's mountain retreat in Vermont to Dorothy Allison's home in northern California. We asked about the genesis of particular novels and stories, how they evolved, and what surprises occurred along the way.

Conducting these interviews—almost fifty in all—was like taking part in a traveling writing workshop. Our subjects shared idiosyncrasies of process, proving in occasionally bizarre ways that there is no formula for writing a good story. One writer collected scenes she saw in her mind's eye and memorized them, sometimes over a period of several years, before holing up for the four months or so it took her to write a book. Another wrote stories in "chunks of the universe that seemed to speak to each other," and then spent hours moving them around to find the right order. Both M. L. and I became better writers, incorporating what we learned into our own work.

Editing the *Story Matters* interviews, I was struck by the fact that very few of the writers we talked to spoke about writing in academic terms. In an attempt to capture this, I wrote:

They spoke like people who worked with their hands. Their subject matter was stuff, flotsam, chunks, slivers, shards, seeds, glimmers, ground, hard-wired obsession. They groped, shifted, leapt, dreamed, coalesced, tunneled their way toward a moment of combustion when they began to sense the bones of a story, see it through some personal lens.

They juggled, calibrated, distilled, juxtaposed, framed, triggered, lumbered, wove, fiddled, embroidered, bridged, crept, tinkered, blasted away, strung along, threaded, accumulated to bring a story into being.

They hobbled language, popped the point of view, considered angles of vision. They worked brick-by-brick, went stepping-stone by stepping-stone. They brought to a boil, folding in details, creating byproducts, considering heft and resonance—all the while listening to the tune of dialogue in their heads.

There's no blueprint for a story, they said. You drill for oil, hang ideas on a clothesline, follow a thin wire through the dark, bounce off walls until, suddenly, stories blossom into metaphor like pop-up books. Stories are like snapping turtles: the words on the page its shell and head above the water, what the author knows beneath, in the hearts and guts and beating paddles of its feet. Stories are tarnish. Perfect, smooth river pebbles. Loose, baggy monsters. Heat and light.

Writers speak differently about finished stories, too. "What did the author *mean*?" English teachers often ask. "What did he *in-*

tend?" When, so often, the writer didn't have a clue.

To many teachers, a story is a finished thing, with a protective shield holding its one single meaning in place. A student's job is to discover that meaning through discussion and research. But writers are less concerned with attaching meaning to aspects of a story than with trying to understand how a story works—how it is *made*. In fact, it's not unusual for writers to miss the meaning in their own finished stories. More than once, during our author interviews, we made an observation about a story's meaning that surprised the writer. Those were great moments. The writer's expression would become bemused. He'd shake his head and confess that this meaning was news to him.

These discoveries were a comfort to me. The literary analysis I learned to practice in literature classes seemed to have little to do with how a story was made. Too often, academia felt (and still feels) like a club to which I can never belong. But writing those two books confirmed that writers *do* see their work differently than most academics—probably because few academics write fiction themselves. They don't know how the creative process works or how it feels.

As I became more confident in my own way of thinking and talking about writing, I was always on the alert for simple language to illuminate how writing works. Writers continued to offer up useful descriptions of process over the years. For example, in one workshop I attended, Tim O'Brien asked again and again, "What is the *aboutness* of the story?" Not theme, but *aboutness*—which makes so much more sense. O'Brien also said, "Don't goose the language." Meaning, don't use fancy language or excessive adverbs or adjectives to tell readers what to think and feel. Make nouns and verbs do the work.

Russell Banks said the same thing in a different way: "The hotter the topic, the cooler the prose." When he said that, I suddenly understood a passage from Martin Cruz Smith's *Polar Star* that made my skin crawl using almost only simple nouns and verbs to describe dozens of eels slithering from a body pulled from the sea.

"There is a peasant in every novelist," F. Scott Fitzgerald wrote, which struck me as strange until it occurred to me that the difference between writing a short story and writing a novel is similar to the difference between tending to a kitchen garden and tending to a whole farm. The day-to-day grind of a novel demands a different kind of energy. Its fluidity, its many moving parts, demand a whole different level of strategy and analysis.

But it was the language I discovered trying to help my students understand how writing worked that helped me the most. "It's like the least common denominator in fractions," I said after numerous attempts to explain what I meant to one girl when I said her sentences were unclear. "When you get to the least common denominator in fractions, there's nowhere else to go with the numbers, right?"

She nodded.

"When your sentence is clear, the words in it mean one thing only. They can't be interpreted any other way."

"*Oh!*" she said.

Oh! I thought. I hadn't seen clarity in that way until I said it.

In a more entertaining illustration of clarity, I asked one student to sit on the table in our writing room and position her limbs as she had positioned her character's limbs in a love scene she had described in her story. She collapsed in laughter when the actual depiction began to resemble a game of Twister. Afterward, all I had to say was "Twister!" when her logistics got out of whack. She knew exactly what I meant.

"Clarity is beauty," Tolstoy said. I'm always on the lookout for practical touchpoints that clarify the elements of good fiction without intimidating language, ways of thinking that enlighten my own creative process and help me welcome students with drive, discipline, and heart into the fold.

Chasing the Muse

One late October afternoon, I was sequestered with a dozen or so students in our cramped creative writing room. They were revising for what seemed like the millionth time the libretto for an opera our performing arts program had won a grant to write and produce. They'd been at it all day—rewriting dialogue, fine-tuning characters and scenes, and squabbling over whether to keep or kill off a trio of girls they'd added to spotlight more female voices.

We were all burned out and cranky. One kid was muttering, Another kid slumped in her chair. One girl's eye was twitching—a chronic ailment over the past few weeks. She was itchy, too—probably breaking out in hives…again. "I hate this," she said. "It doesn't feel creative, at all."

"I hate to tell you," I said. "But this is *exactly* what creative feels like."

At that moment, nobody but me was amused. But when it was

all over—the libretto finished, the opera produced and well-reviewed in the local press—I think (hope) most of the group would have agreed with their fellow librettist who observed, "Writing the libretto was the most fun, horrible, challenging, amazing thing I've ever been a part of."

As my student librettists discovered, along with every other creative writing student I've ever had, being creative is fun, but it's also frustrating, surprising, discouraging, exhilarating, satisfying—and terribly misunderstood. Someone who puts clothes together in interesting ways is said to be creative. So is a Pulitzer Prize–winning novelist. Our culture uses the word *creative* in so many different ways that its meaning has become slippery and obscured.

Creativity is a process, not a trait. The most useful definition I've ever found is this one, from Erik Maisel's *Staying Sane in the Arts*: "People are artistically creative when they love what they are doing, know what they are doing and actively engage in the tasks we call art making. The three elements of creativity are thus, loving, knowing, and doing; or heart, mind, and hands; or, as Buddhist teaching has it, great faith, great question, and great courage."

Real writers...write.

And write and write and write.

They are people who make things with their hands, humble and proficient in their craft. They follow their hearts, addressing the unanswerable questions of human existence with determination and courage. Good stories are, in Maisel's words, "the encounter of an intensely conscious mind with his or her world."

Inspiration comes most often in process. If you're lucky, it will arrive—and, for a little while, the words will come easily. You'll be lost in their flow. If inspiration doesn't come, that day's work will be tedious and slow. But you'll put words on the page nonetheless, each one a small step toward your finished story.

So, stop chasing the muse.

The muse is you.

What They Said

Kurt Vonnegut's Blessing

DURING THOSE TWENTY YEARS OF LONGING BUT not trying to write, sometimes what felt like the ghost of a story would come to me: an image I couldn't forget, or the sense of a character with problems that intrigued me. But no whole, full-blown story ever presented itself. Finally, I started writing anyway, with little idea where a story was going, constantly getting stuck, fearful that I'd never be able to figure out how to do it right. I had to coax every single story out of my brain using a series of tricks I developed—poor substitutes, I thought, for imagination.

Then I had the good fortune to hear Kurt Vonnegut do a Q&A with a creative-writing class at a local university. It was in the 1980s, when you could still smoke in public places, and he sat in the classroom, chain-smoking, smushing the butts into the chalk tray, patiently answering questions he'd no doubt been asked a million times before. Finally, one student, after pontificating for a while about Vonnegut's work, asked him to explain how he wrote stories. "It must have gotten a lot easier for you over the years," the student supposed.

Vonnegut gave the kid a long look, then took a drag from his cigarette. The room was dead quiet. The students leaned forward in their seats, waiting to hear the secret of how he'd gotten to the place where writing stories was *easy*. But instead, what he said was, "If I knew how a story was going to turn out, why would I write it?"

I'd never been so relieved in my life!

I had always assumed that having imagination meant that stories came into your head like gifts and all you had to do was write them down. But based on that definition, Kurt Vonnegut didn't have an imagination at all! That could mean only one thing: My definition must be wrong. If Kurt Vonnegut didn't know—didn't even *want* to know—how a story was going to turn out when he started it, maybe I was on the right track, after all.

My understanding of imagination evolved from that moment. Like creativity, it is a process, not a trait—no more than asking, "What if?" again and again in every phase of discovering and writing a story. It's having an open mind, an infinite curiosity about the world we live in and the people who share it with us—*all of them*—so that the "what ifs" you ask are not limited by a narrow vision.

Recently, a friend of mine who writes speculative fiction, added another question to the mix: "Why not?" Good writers live in a constant state of observation. They eavesdrop. They sit in cafés or on park benches or beach blankets, notebooks at the ready to record a detail they don't want to forget. They're curious about *everything*. Always asking, "Why not?" and "Why?" Always wondering what might be, or what could have been.

Paul Klee's Sketchbook

I LOVE PAUL KLEE'S PAINTINGS. THEY'RE SO simple at first glance, it's common to hear someone scoff, "A child could have done that!" But if you look long enough, almost transparent dabs of burnt sienna and eucalyptus green give way to long rectangles topped with triangles, becoming a desert or a faraway walled city—so evocative that for a moment, you're standing in the hot dry air under the bleached sky. You can almost hear the *muezzin*'s call to prayer.

Or, what first seems like a real thing—a crude black outline of a house with a tilted roofline set on a mosaic background of thousands of tiny squares—can shift and suddenly become nothing more than a tilted triangle. In fact, the painting might be no more than a study of triangles and almost-triangles. Then there are the countless color studies. Blocks of what seem like random color marching across a canvas. That's it, you think. Just that. Until you look long enough to hear them singing.

The more I look at a painting by Paul Klee, the more I listen to the colors, the more I'm drenched with emotion, unbalanced by the intensity, the mystery of how color and shape can make that happen. The whimsy underpinned by strangeness and wonder.

Once, entering a retrospective of Klee's work, I couldn't wait to see room after room of his paintings. But what caught my eye was a glass case with an open sketchbook. *Cool*, I thought, expecting it to show studies with colors, patterns, and images later incorporated into paintings. But what the open sketchbook revealed was a drawing of a farmhouse and the landscape surrounding it—so perfectly rendered that it might have been a photograph. It turns out, Paul Klee had a degree in fine arts, and his passion for color led him to endless experiments in color and form. Over time, he developed his own color theory, which he taught to students at the Bauhaus art school in Germany.

"Rules are made to be broken," artists often say. Which is true enough. The best artists broke the rules of preceding generations to create something wholly new—which then generated a whole new set of rules for subsequent generations to break. But like Klee, most of those artists had mastered the rules first. They broke them because the rules couldn't accommodate what they imagined.

There are rules for writing fiction, too—guidelines we use to talk about aspects of the craft that must be mastered to write a good story, like dialogue, voice, characterization, setting, plot, and scene. You might, as I did, write a publishable first novel by some combination of instinct and dumb luck. But it's very unlikely to happen twice. Twelve years passed between the publication of my first and second novels. It took me that long to understand how the rules of fiction worked well enough to employ the unselfconsciously. Twelve years to earn the right to abandon them when a story insisted on going its own way.

Piero's Byzantine Hats

ABOUT TWENTY YEARS AGO, I FELL MADLY in love with the paintings and frescoes of the early Renaissance painter, Piero della Francesca. I yearned for even an inkling of insight into how he made them. I wanted to *write* about how he made them. But to accomplish this, I would need to understand the nature of visual ideas, how they evolve, and how they're the same as and different from ideas for stories. I needed to hold a paintbrush in my hand, lower it to a palette of color, feel the surprise of a brush stroke on canvas, and consider its implications.

Piero was a regional artist. Although most of the important artists of his time gravitated to Florence or Rome, he spent most of his working life in and around Umbria, where he was born. This interested me. So, I applied for a grant to study painting at Art Workshop International in Assisi—in the heart of Piero's world.

I was thrilled when my grant application was accepted. But when I arrived in Assisi, watching the taxi that had deposited me in front of the Hotel Giotto make its way back down the hill, I had a moment of sheer terror. I couldn't draw. I couldn't paint. Yet, here I was among all these...*artists*. I was about to make a colossal fool of myself.

But there was B., a woman in her eighties dressed in a voluminous black dress, her salt-and-pepper hair in a Louise Brooks bob. "You must be Barbara Shoup!" she said, engulfing me in a hug. I felt, in that instant, part of the family of art. For B., the fact that I had zero experience as an artist posed no problem at all. "Art is all around you," she said. "Look. You'll find it."

I had expected…I don't know. Lessons, maybe. But B. set me loose to discover my work with absolute confidence that I would find it. The next day, wandering Assisi, anxiously wondering how in the world I was going to come up with an idea, I came upon St. Francis's cloak in a glass case in the basilica museum. I looked at it a long time—its simple design, its tattered geometry of black and gray and white patches—marveling that St. Francis himself had worn this, had walked the streets I'd walked to reach this place where I was standing now. Eventually, I drifted toward the exit. I bought a postcard of the cloak and left the basilica. But I couldn't stop thinking about it.

So—still with no idea I thought worthy of *art*—I went back to the studio, enlarged the image on the postcard, and traced the pattern of patches onto a piece of heavy drawing paper. I opened my brand-new tubes of acrylic paint and painted the cloak. But instead of using black, gray, and white, I opted for blues, pinks, golds, and greens—the colors, I realized only later, of the early Renaissance. The transformation of one color into another with just a dab of different pigment delighted me; the drag of the paint beneath my brush brought a physical pleasure I couldn't have imagined. Time went by. Hours. I was lost, exactly the way I'm lost when writing a story.

I was quite pleased with my version of St. Francis's cloak. But—like so many of my writing students—I felt I should apologize for being, well, a student. And wasn't what I'd done sort of cheating?

"Absolutely not!" B. said. "It's wonderful. It's art. You're making art from what's around you."

I felt as if I'd just painted a masterpiece.

I moved on to the Byzantine hats in Piero's fresco cycle, "Legend of the True Cross"—hats that some art historians believe Piero saw in Florence worn by delegates from Constantinople attending a symposium on the reunification of the church. Some hats looked like dinner plates, some looked like funnels, like mushrooms, like crowns. There were simple skull caps, pancake hats, slouchy berets. Tall hats with forked points that looked like knife blades, hats that curved upward from the base, so unwieldy you half worry they'll tip right off the wearer's head into your hands.

I spent hours one morning looking at the hats, tracing the shapes onto stiff paper again and again, cutting them out into templates until I had a few dozen to work with. I made a blue wash on my paper; then, when it was dry, I spent an hour moving the hats around it until I found just the right arrangement. I outlined them lightly in pencil and painted them.

I was heady with hats. For the rest of the two weeks, I painted them falling like rain on stone walls and among twisty cypresses; in the foreground of medieval arches; surrounding a rough likeness of Piero's face; dancing, *Fantasia*-like, across the canvas.

Painting those hats made me so happy.

Maybe I could be a painter *and* a writer, I thought…until it occurred to me that this was a reprise of the instinct and dumb luck phenomenon I experienced as a novice writer. Painting would be no different. To become a writer, I had to learn about plot and character, setting and scene. If I wanted to become a painter, I would have to learn about color, shape, and line. I'd have to learn about the properties of paint. I'd have to allow myself to paint badly until I could forget what I knew and paint without self-consciousness.

Becoming a serious artist of any kind is like falling in love. There's the thrill of desire, the delight in being lost in the company of your beloved. But in time, the exhilaration gives way to little tensions and disappointments, deal-breaker problems that must be resolved. If you survive that second phase, you'll have learned that love is work—which is by no means the end of joy. If your love is writing, you'll always find joy in the wonder of words, in the sweet echo of excitement in each beginning, and in those moments when you see all you've put into the long journey of becoming a writer reflected in the depth and resonance of your stories.

Hemingway's Iceberg

A WRITER FRIEND AND I WERE CHATTING about various book ideas we were considering when he told me he was thinking about a road trip book set in 1964, in which a teenage boy falls in love with *On the Road*, finds out that Jack Kerouac lives in St. Petersburg, Florida, and takes off to find him.

"I love that idea," I said, adding (only half-joking), "If you ever decide you don't want it, can I have it?"

He laughed. "Sure," he said.

Five or so years later, over lunch, he said, "Hey, I'm not going to use that Kerouac idea. So, if you want it, you can have it."

Cool! I thought.

I couldn't wait to start the book.

I started researching Kerouac, and found myself especially drawn in by the last years of his life. By 1964, he was a wreck, an alcoholic living with his mother in a crummy little prefab house with cats prowling in the yard. At times he was tender, at times cruel. He hated the fame he'd worked so hard for and hid from it when he could.

I really wanted to put Kerouac in a story and see what he would do, but I couldn't get a fix on the characters I'd inherited from my friend. They just wouldn't come alive. No character appeared, as characters sometimes do, to show me the way.

Time passed. I worked on other things.

Then my sister J. was diagnosed with terminal brain cancer.

Her only symptom had been vertigo, which her family doctor had treated as an inner-ear infection. Now it was as if her whole body had been shocked into responding to what was happening inside her head. By the time I got to her house, she was in bed, alternately burning up and freezing. Her teeth chattered. She was gray. Her eyes were screwed shut because her head hurt so much. Her husband and two teenage sons watched helplessly as she suffered. Finally, the pain got so bad, we took her to the hospital.

For all of the next day, she lay there, rigid, her eyes still shut against the pain. Now and then, she'd make a small, whimpering sound. We put cool cloths on her forehead, held her hands, raised a glass of water and guided the straw to her lips.

"It's all right. You'll be all right," we told her.

But she was never all right again. Shattered, the rest of us entered the long, dark tunnel of her illness, doing our best to care for her and for each other. Her death, fifteen months after the diagnosis, brought both heartbreak and relief. That morning, it began to snow. As two men from the funeral home zipped her up in a bag and took her away, I stood at a window, watching the flakes fall. So cold, the whole world disappearing beneath them. But beautiful, too. A red cardinal landed on the branch of a nearby tree, setting off its own tiny snowfall, and it seemed like a sign—though I couldn't have said of what.

A few months later, a girl with straw blond hair and turquoise eyes standing behind the counter of a diner appeared in my mind's eye. My sister, at eighteen.

She's the girl, I thought.

And it occurred to me that my main character's flight from the life he and everyone else believed he was meant to live could be a desperate attempt to right the shift in his world that had occurred at his mother's death. It wouldn't just be a road trip. It would be a road trip fueled by grief. The boy's yearning would match the restless yearning in my own heart, and might help me better understand what it had been like for my two teenage nephews to lose their mom.

I still miss my sister more than I can say. But writing *Looking for Jack Kerouac* helped me come to terms with her death and to remember her in a way that doesn't make me unbearably sad. It also taught me the difference between a good idea and *my* good idea.

"If a writer of prose knows enough about what he is writing about, he may omit things that he knows and the reader, if the writer is writing truly enough, will have a feeling of those things as strongly as though the writer had stated them," Ernest Hemingway wrote. "The dignity of movement of an iceberg is due to only one-eighth of it being above water." In other words, as the grandeur of the iceberg's tip is dependent on what cannot be seen beneath, the power of a story is dependent on what the writer knows but does not include.

I offer my corollary to this theory: The power of a story is due not only to what the writer knows about the story, but to how much is at stake, personally, in writing it. That is, the question that fuels the plot of a good story comes from the writer's struggle with at least one of her unanswerable questions, and writing that story offers the possibility of revealing insight that relates to a crucial issue in her real life.

Captain Fiction's Assault

GORDON LISH, A.K.A. CAPTAIN FICTION, SWEPT INTO the room decked out in full safari regalia, pith helmet included. He took his place at the front of the room and gazed out at us, his prey: fifty or so writers crammed so close together in rows of uncomfortable mismatched chairs that we could smell the morning coffee on each other's breath. We'd paid dearly to attend the twelve-hour workshop, which, we knew from Lish's reputation, would be grueling, hellish—sadistic, even. Each of us would read aloud from our manuscript until Lish got bored, stopped us, and made a lesson of everything wrong with what we'd written. The only breaks would be one half hour for lunch and another for dinner. Bathroom breaks were allowed but discouraged.

Why did I—why would *anyone*—sign up for this? For one simple reason: Lish was a respected literary editor who loved discovering new writers. He was legendary for launching and championing their careers. In fact, we soon learned, he had discovered one writer sitting among us in the audience: D., a chic North Shore woman in her mid-forties. "*Here* is a serious writer," Lish said, pointing at D. "A writer willing to put herself on the line." He went on to commend her courage. "You have to write your secrets," he explained. "The things you're most ashamed of, the things you don't want *anyone* to know about you." And D., he said, who was working on a story based on a sexual relationship between her children, had done just that.

I sat through the next hours with increasing dread as Lish shot down writer after writer. The tension in the room became almost unbearable. Thinking back on the experience, I can see myself in that room, lifting my manuscript to read when my turn came. I can see Lish looking at me, feel his predatory stare. Then my memory goes blank. At which sentence did Lish cut me off? What did he say was wrong with that sentence? How did he use my mistakes to illustrate what a writer should *never* do? I don't know. All I remember is the burn of anger and humiliation inside me—how I couldn't look up until he'd moved on to the next person.

Lish was a bully—an egomaniac so in love with his own image that he kept that ridiculous pith helmet on all day. Nonetheless, once the shock of the experience wore off, I began to remember things he said. Like:

"Suppose every sentence has a weight—say, ten. If there are ten words in a sentence, each word weighs one. For every word you take out, the ones left weigh more."

"Each sentence should follow naturally, inevitably, from the preceding sentences."

"A sentence should attack in its unexpectedness and linguistic drama."

"Reduce your strategy to the most urgent sentence you can possibly find."

"Writing, you must feel as if you're grabbing the reader by the lapel and saying, 'You have to read this or I will die!'"

I have a vivid memory of Lish scribbling this Hemingway quote on the blackboard: "The world breaks everyone and afterward many are strong in the broken places. But those that will not break it kills. It kills the very good and the very gentle and the very brave impartially. If you are none of these you can be sure it will kill you too but there will be no special hurry."

"Alliteration," Lish bellowed, chalking lines from one B to the next, crisscrossing them across the paragraph. He did the same with each K. Going so fast the chalk splintered, he made more lines to show us the pattern of assonance, dissonance, rhythm, repetition—and how, in the end, the crisscrossing lines of each element were so close together you could barely see the sentences beneath them. "Your sentences should create an invisible grid on the page, holding the reader in the story," he said.

Much as I hate to admit it, that brutal day with Gordon Lish changed the way I thought about writing. It changed the way I *wrote*. I now understand—and even appreciate—his singlemindedness, his fervent, some might say maniacal, belief in the power of a perfect sentence. Writing was his religion. He was the god.

Also true: Although being discovered and championed by such a powerful and charismatic editor might be a wonderful thing, it will depend to some degree on writing according to his personal standards for the rest of your career. So be careful. Not being discovered and championed by an influential editor doesn't mean your work isn't as good as the work chosen. It may, in fact, be better—just different.

You *can* learn from a bully, but don't take his—or any—criticism personally. Stay cool. Take what seems useful and put the rest out of your mind. When you feel intimidated, sit up straight and look him in the eye.

Remember who you are.

The Diary of Samuel Pepys

Although I was an avid reader as a teenager, all too often, reading "literature" in high school seemed like trying to read a foreign language. Although *Beowulf* did inspire our senior class homecoming float (titled "Dragon Down the Archers"), none of what we read seemed to have much to do with *me*. So, I barely slogged through *Sir Gawain and the Green Knight*, *Piers Plowman*, and the Troubadour poets. The prospect of "mystery plays" sparked some hope, but they turned out to be just Bible stories. Our ancient English teacher droned on about the life of Edmund Spenser—and, worse, read breathily from *The Faerie Queen*, eliciting guffaws from the boys in the back row.

I should have liked *The Canterbury Tales*, but I didn't. Everyone is supposed to like Shakespeare, because he's…Shakespeare. And who knows? I might have liked *Macbeth* if we hadn't spent days reading it aloud, going up and down the rows, each person reading a single speech. Plus, it was spring by then, and I was afflicted by serious senioritis. All I could think of was getting out of English class, out of high school, out of town—fleeing everything familiar to me and starting my "real" life.

Then we got to *The Diary of Samuel Pepys*.

Here was something about the lives of real people, full of triumph and disappointment, joy and grief, kindness and cruelty, jokes and slights. What they wore, what they ate, where they lived and worked, who they loved and who they only endured. I read the excerpt in our textbook like a novel, delighted at every turn by its gossipy tone and by the language itself—which, for some reason, I found hilarious. Things like:

"Anon comes Mr. Andrews to see and sing with me."

"Thence to Whitehall."

"She, poor wretch, hath a mind to stay a little longer, and I cannot blame her, considering what a life she will through her own folly lead when she comes home again."

"At this Committee, unknown to me, comes my Lord of Sandwich."

"My wife was in London when he came thither."

Anon! Thence! Poor wretch! Comes my Lord of Sandwich! Came thither! I loved the way the words rolled off my tongue. And I loved the assignment our teacher gave us: Write a diary entry of a day in your own life in the style of Samuel Pepys. I dashed mine off, then did another and another, supplying diary entries to classmates who didn't have a clue about how to do it themselves. I got an A on every one.

The Diary of Samuel Pepys woke me from the torpor of senior English. It was my introduction to voice—the first time I realized that writing had flavor, and that this flavor came from the personality of the writer, the way he saw the world, and the language of his time. Although Pepys' use of language was completely different from my own, I knew intuitively that he wrote just as he spoke. I hadn't known you could do that. Or, to be more specific, I hadn't known you could write like that and end up in an English literature book.

Unfortunately, I forgot this lesson for a long time. I struggled through freshman literature in college, waking only to weird assignments, like, "Choose ten well-known contemporary figures and place each one in the appropriate circle of Dante's hell."

When teaching myself to write, I tried too hard to be literary. It took me forever to stop worrying about developing my style and trusting my own voice.

What I learned from Samuel Pepys—and promptly forgot—was that style is born of who you are: the way you see the world, the language available to you, the stuff inside your head, and the details life offers up day-to-day. It's reflected in the length, rhythm, and complexity of your sentences; your word choice; your use of metaphor and sensory language. Talking about how a story works, people often lump its voice, dialogue, tone, mood, and style together. But they are not the same thing at all!

The voice of a story is its personality—as complex as a person's personality, a combination of characteristics or qualities that makes it difficult to pin down.

Dialogue is characters talking in the story.

A story's tone is the writer's attitude toward the material explored in the story. It's *never* expressed outright, but in very specific details, clues, that guide readers toward seeing the situation as the writer does.

Mood is the atmosphere the writer creates in the story through careful use of words. A brutal story might be told in a staccato rhythm, using a lot of words with hard consonants. Mood is not created by a pile-up of adjectives or adverbs. It's created with sensory detail that brings readers into the story, makes them feel how the characters feel. Mood can change within a story, but when it does be sure to create a transition so the reader won't be jarred by it.

Style is the instinctive use of language that creates a writer's own unique voice and adapts to the nature of every story they write. For example, Eudora Welty's "Why I Live at the P.O." and "A Worn Path" couldn't be more different, yet we instantly recognize them as hers.

Your stories could be as different "I Want to Hold Your Hand" and "I Am the Walrus" by the Beatles, and there would *still* be no question about who wrote them. Just as we recognize good musicians when we hear their songs, we recognize good writers when we read their stories.

"You do not create a style," Katherine Anne Porter said. "You work, and develop yourself; your style is an emanation of your own being."

Muriel Sparks' Consolation

DURING THE SUMMER OF 1985, WHEN MY oldest daughter graduated from high school, we took a family trip to London. Back then, Laura Ashley dresses were all the rage. So, in a haze of excitement, my two daughters and I visited the Laura Ashley store in Kensington. By coincidence, everything was on sale. Prices were astonishingly low, so we fell into a frenzy—grabbing frocks from the racks, scrambling to the fitting rooms, trying them on, keeping some, abandoning others, and repeating the whole process all over again. Finally, we decided which dresses we wanted. I carried them to the cashier, heaved them onto the counter, and then rifled through my shoulder bag for the small purse with my money in it.

It wasn't there.

The purse had been stolen.

After considerable reflection, all I could figure out was that the thief had snaked an arm under the fitting-room partition and plucked the purse from my open bag, which I had stupidly set on the floor. That meant the thief was a woman. Plus, the store was in a posh neighborhood—meaning she had to look enough like the other women in the store to escape notice.

It got weirder. Along with my cash and traveler's checks, our passports had been in the purse. It was too late that day to go to the American Embassy to see about replacing them. So, the next morning, I went there early, right when it opened, steeled for a major ordeal. Incredibly, the lady at the desk smiled when I told her my name. "The purse was turned in at Victoria Station," she said. "You can pick it up at the Lost and Found there any time."

Predictably, the cash and traveler's checks were gone. But the passports were there. So was my credit card and a photo of my two-year old nephew mowing the lawn with his toy lawnmower. And there was something else: When I travel, I always jot down money conversions on a little index card for handy reference. The index card was still in the purse—but the thief had torn it in half and put back in its place, as if to say, "You won't be needing *this* anymore."

I was angry, of course. But that detail thrilled me. I knew I would get a story out of it—and, in time, I did. "A Woman Like Myself" begins:

I watch two women approach my flat, surely high school English teachers from America, and think how pleased they will the next time they read "Belgravia" in a novel, to remember the stately white row houses, the bright flowerboxes, the elegant wrought iron fences. A door opening, a woman stepping out of it dressed in a wool plaid skirt, wearing a Burberry raincoat and carrying a green Harrods bag. A woman they believe to be as English as the Queen.

The story follows the narrator through the morning to the moment when the bitterness she feels about the collapse of her marriage and the desertion of her daughters is revealed in an act of theft in that same Laura Ashley store full of tourists—wives, mothers, daughters. She rips "my" index card in half to celebrate having spoiled someone else's day.

Something I love about being a writer is how unfortunate experiences morph into stories. How even grief yields information necessary to make a work of fiction real.

"Nothing is lost," novelist Muriel Spark observed. The promise of a story as a place to put to rest the things that make us angry or dispirited or sad—or happy, for that matter—is a consolation.

All that emotion! Where do people who aren't writers put it? How do they let it go?

Edith Wharton's Grave

I'VE NEVER MET A GOOD WRITER WHO doesn't read—*obsessively*. They'll read the back of a cereal box if that's the only reading matter available. I know, because I'm that way myself. In fact, I'm *such* an obsessive reader that when my second daughter was born, I spent most of my time in the hospital blazing through a juicy James Michener novel, and every time the nurse brought the baby to my room, I'd glance up from the book and think, *Can't she wait?*

What you read is not a moral issue. If someone claims there's a certified list of books (mostly by dead people) that every aspiring writer must read, don't believe it. Some, but not all, writers read the classics. But they also read current literary fiction. And memoirs and biographies. And history books, science books—really, nonfiction of all kinds. Not to mention science fiction, fantasy, chick-lit, romance, thrillers, crime novels—the list goes on.

Writers read for knowledge and for insight. They read for escape—for the pure pleasure of words.

And, they read to learn how to write.

The more you read, the more you will be amazed by how often books appear on your writing path at exactly the right moment to teach you something you need to know—even if that something is what you should never *ever* do in your own stories. Most of the time, what you learn from a book comes to you like a gift—one of those "Oh!" moments in which something you've been puzzling over suddenly and for no logical reason clicks into place. But sometimes it's worth taking a deeper look at a book or story you love, just to see what it might teach you.

I learned this when I was invited to participate in a local library lecture series that featured writers talking about a favorite short story from a writer's point of view. "Sure," I said. "I'll do it." I picked my all-time favorite story: Edith Wharton's "Roman Fever."

This will be easy, I thought. I would just read some literary criticism. Bone up on Wharton's life. How hard could that be? But I put it off and put it off. Pretty soon, the talk was just a month away—three weeks of which I would be traveling in France.

I put a copy of the story in my suitcase, along with Wharton's book, *The Writing of Fiction,* and prayed I'd be struck by inspiration while I was away. Knowing Edith Wharton had lived much of her adult life in France, I also leafed through a biography I'd read about her, jotting down places she'd been that I might visit while I was there. If nothing else, I could eat up a bunch of time talking about that.

One entry on the list was Wharton's grave in the town of Versailles, a quick train ride from Paris. When I arrived, I approached the clerk at the station's information desk. She smiled, her yellow highlighter poised to mark the route to Versailles Palace—the destination of most tourists she encountered—on a paper map.

"Non," I said. Then, in my fractured high school French, I attempted to explain that I wanted directions for the town cemetery.

The clerk gave one of those little shrugs the French are famous for. Then she pointed at the paper map. *"Le cimitière est ici,"* she said, drawing a yellow line to show the way.

Map in hand, I walked about a mile along a congested thoroughfare lined with small businesses and shabby cafés. Then I crossed to the cemetery, which was marked by a stone gateway. Near the entrance was a small office. I went inside. It was dingy and gray, an ancient oak card catalogue spanning one whole wall. At the desk sat a clerk in a haze of cigarette smoke.

"Bonjour," I said. Then, in my poor French, I attempted to ask him where I could find the grave of the American author Edith Wharton.

He looked at me, uncomprehending.

I tried again. *"Auteur Americaine?"* I said. "Edith Wharton?"

Still lost, the man splayed his hands apologetically. Then he slid a piece of paper toward me and offered me a pen. I gave up on *auteur* and wrote only her name.

The man peered at it. "Adeeth Wharetone," he said. *"Elle est Americaine?"*

"*Oui,*" I said.

"Ah!" His face lit up in a smile. "*Famille!*"

He looked so approving of my having come all this way to visit the grave of a relative that I didn't have the heart—or, frankly, the linguistic ability—to tell him he was wrong. Besides, I quite liked the idea of being related to Edith Wharton. So, I said, "*Oui!*"

He turned to the card catalogue, cigarette smoke trailing behind him, and soon produced a yellowed index card. On it, "Edith Wharton" was written in beautiful script, browned with age. Beneath her name, in smaller script, was the date and place of her burial. The clerk pointed toward the widest path, straight up the center of a hill, then waved vaguely to the right as he spoke. Apparently, I looked confused, because he stopped mid-sentence and laughed.

"*Allons-y!*" he said. I followed him outside. He hopped on a moped, motioned for me to follow, and I trotted after him as he putt-putted up the hill. He angled right at the top and rolled to a stop near the cemetery's back wall. "*Voila!*" he said with a grand gesture. "Aideeth Wharetone!" Then he gave me a little salute and zoomed away.

It was a simple monument: a flat, rectangular granite marker on a raised planting bed about two feet high, surrounded by a low stone wall. The marker featured a raised cross and a Latin phrase carved into the stone that translated roughly to, "The cross is our one hope." Also carved into the stone were Wharton's married and maiden names and the dates of her birth and death. The marker was weathered—mottled with bird-droppings and mold. Some of the carved letters and numbers had grown so indistinct that I had to feel them to be certain what they were. The planting bed was overgrown with weeds and littered with bits of broken stone and glass.

The energy I had expended to make myself understood by the cemetery clerk and the quick trot up the hill had made me tired. Now, finding the grave untended made me sad. I sat down on the low stone wall around where Edith Wharton lay, thinking of the marvelous stories she had made out of her rich and painful life. I imagined her propped up in bed, dressed in an elegant bed jacket, her writing board on her lap as it was most mornings. I saw her motoring through the countryside with Henry James in the afternoons; in the evenings, entertaining friends to whom she had passionate attachments. Far from home myself, I thought of the pleasure she had taken from travel, and of how she had made use of disappointing, even disastrous excursions in her work. It seemed terribly wrong to me that she had ended up in this ugly place—forgotten and alone.

I sat with her for a long time, as if that might make a difference.

Then, spurred suddenly to action, I knelt and weeded her grave. I cleared away the broken stones and glass. I marched down the hill to the florist's shop nearby and bought two pink begonia plants, five *francs* each. Back in the cemetery, as I carried them up the path to Wharton's grave, I encountered a stout old woman.

"*Bonjour, Madame,*" she said, smiling approvingly at the begonias.

"*Bonjour, Madame,*" I sang out, the virtuous daughter.

The soil was dry and caked hard. It took a long time to dig a hole with the shard of glass I'd found. I was so pleased with myself, so absorbed with digging and planting, that it wasn't until

I finished the job and stepped back to survey the result that I saw how absurd my efforts had been. Wharton had loved flowers; she had written wonderfully of her own garden and of the gardens of others. It was now obvious to me that her grave had been designed to burst with blooms. My two begonias suddenly looked small and sad—mean, even.

They might have seemed even smaller, even sadder, even meaner to me at that moment if I hadn't remembered Wharton's dry sense of humor. That and her sharp sense of irony often surprised people who expected to meet a character as stuffy and humorless as some of those she created. I decided that my flowers were a detail Wharton would have appreciated. Later, I would even dare imagine that she might have used those pitiful flowers, and the visit of a fellow writer to her grave, in a story.

Of course, none of this assisted me in my interpretation of "Roman Fever." So, for the rest of my time in France, I kept the story in my daypack and pulled it out whenever a moment presented itself. I read "Roman Fever" in countless cafés over coffee and croissants, on the Metro, on trains traveling to Chartres, Giverny, and Rouen. I read it on a bench in the Luxembourg Garden and stretched out on the grass in the shadow of the Eiffel Tower. I read it in bed each night as I drifted exhausted into sleep.

Every time I read it I saw something new. The margins of the story were crowded with my notes, the body marked with underlining, circled phrases, exclamation points, arrows, and stars. In time, after who knows how many readings, it was as if the skeleton of the story revealed itself. I began to understand how "Roman Fever" worked. How it moved. I saw how masterfully Wharton crab-walked the reader toward one of the most surprising and perfect endings in American fiction.

A good literary critic might have recognized these things and pointed them out. But reading that criticism wouldn't have given me the pleasure of discovery or the visceral jolt of understanding that showed me how to make my own work better. I'm not saying literary criticism of a story isn't valuable. I'm just saying that if you want to be a writer, the story itself will teach you more.

Fiction 101

Before and After

I MET S. ON THE FIRST DAY of my freshman year of college. I was sitting at a table in the Commons with a bunch of girls I'd just met when he and some fraternity brothers—including two pledges from my hometown—strode up. S. was stocky, like a football player. He had curly red hair cropped short and freckles turned copper by the sun and wore thick black glasses. He was dressed in the uniform of the time: khaki pants, oxford button-down shirt, navy London Fog jacket, loafers with no socks. Later, I learned that as they had entered the Commons, one of the boys from my hometown had cocked his head toward me and said, "Hey, I know that girl!" and S. had asked him to introduce us. "Why?" I've asked him countless times since then.

He always says, "I just knew."

It wasn't love at first sight for me. In fact—full disclosure—I thought one of his friends was way cuter. But S. was so...*there*. Present. He asked me to a party happening the next night, and I said, yes. Then, as he moved on through the Commons, I descended into a state of mortification. Had it been a joke? Had those guys I knew set it up? Would he show up? Would he *not* show up? Which would be worse?

The next afternoon, he came to my dorm—not quite as sure of himself as he'd been the day before—to make sure I really wanted to go. And then I knew I did.

Here I am on that first date as Jane, the main character in *An American Tune:*

> *The party was in the attic of the Sigma Chi house, where no girls were supposed to be. James Brown was blaring on the stereo. People were dancing, the floor slick with spilled beer. Along one wall, there was a row of battered couches where sorority girls perched, laughing, on their dates' laps. The room was smoky, close. The red tips of cigarettes glittered in the dark corners.*
>
> *"Watch out." That's what Karen Conklin had said the night before, when they were getting acquainted and Jane told her that she and Bridget had been invited to a fraternity party. "Those boys are wild," Karen said. "John—that's my boyfriend—he told me they ask out freshman girls, get them drunk and then—well, you know."*
>
> *But Jane nursed a single beer most of the evening, and Tom didn't seem to notice. He talked to her. He held his cigarette between his thumb and index finger, taking deep drags. He blew the smoke out evenly, careful as a little kid trying to make perfect soap bubbles. He talked about school, about the guys he lived with. About mornings, hunting with his father—how the fog sat in little pockets in*

the hollows and his feet went numb with cold and time stopped. He talked for so long it seemed he'd been saving these things all his life, waiting for the moment she would walk into it so he could tell them to her.

Later, in his room, he pulled her toward him. Now, Jane thought. She hadn't dated much in high school; she'd never had a real boyfriend. Mostly, she had obsessed over certain unattainable boys, shocked speechless on the rare occasion one of them ever said a word to her. She had no idea what Tom expected of her now, or what she would say or do if it seemed wrong to her. She tried to concentrate on the bookshelves in the built-in desk they leaned against. Fat, leather-bound business textbooks. A Farewell to Arms, The Catcher in the Rye. *The books made her feel a little better, but the dark shadow of the bed still frightened her.*

He kissed her—a good kiss. She knew enough to know that. Then in what was almost like a dance step, he pushed her away so that they stood apart, just holding hands. "Don't be scared, Jane. I'm not in any hurry here."

"I'm not scared," she said.

"Yeah, you are. Hey, I don't bring girls up here all the time. This isn't a game with me."

He lit a cigarette and blew smoke rings that dissolved into the room's gray corners. "Come on. Smile."

And she did, in spite of herself.

"Good." He smiled back.

She laughed a little, drifted over to the window. Outside the streetlamps shone, and she could hear the music from the party. She felt him move closer. He stood behind her, not touching her, but so close that she could feel the rhythm of his breathing. There was the faint scent of tobacco mixed with the scent of English Leather. They stood there for a long time. Jane thought that if she raised her arm, his arm would raise, too. If she made a quick feint sideways, he would follow. She let out a deep sigh, and he encircled her.

Boom. Just like that, I had stepped into another life. Literally overnight, I'd gone from being an unhappy high school student, miserable with my family, living in an ugly post-war suburb, to a college girl with a boyfriend, engaged with her studies and social life, living on a campus so beautiful it seemed like a dream. It wasn't perfect—life never is. I worried that S. would wake up some day and realize how uncool I really was. I worried about how much college cost, knowing my parents couldn't really afford it. I dreaded having to go home for Thanksgiving. I dreaded bringing S. home with me, which I knew I'd have to do eventually, because I'd kept how poor we were a secret from him. And I'd kept him a secret from my parents, too, as if telling them would somehow drag me back into their orbit.

I didn't know it then, but meeting S. spoke to my unanswerable question about family: *Why did it have to be that way?* Right from the start, I recognized the possibility that life with him—a family, if we had one—wouldn't be the way life with my family had been. I just had to pay attention to the voice in my head saying, "Don't be stupid. Don't let this go."

Dozens of scenes come to mind when I think of that time— not all happy or romantic, by any means. Some of the scenes are flashbacks to the time *before* we met—underpinning and explaining my awkwardness in the new relationship, my fear of pretty much everything. I trusted S. That was all I knew for sure. More than fifty years later, I still do.

We all have before-and-after moments in life, moments when something shifts, changing the way we live in the world. They're not always as dramatic and obvious as the one I just described. Sometimes, it's only looking back that we see a moment for what it was. But, large or small, these moments have repercussions ripe with tension, conflict, and emotion. They're always accompanied by vivid memories—scenes. And scenes are the building blocks of good fiction.

Like most fiction writers, I consciously or subconsciously mine my life for stories. I only realized after the novels were finished that I'd explored the moment I met S. in four different novels, imagining lives I might have led if things had turned out differently.

What if I'd gotten caught up in an act of political violence that severed the relationship while we were still young? (*An American Tune.*)

What if S. had gone to Vietnam, was injured in a mine blast that disabled him, and broke up with me when he got back because he believed he had to start all over? (Early drafts of *Stranded in Harmony.*)

What if S. had revealed a secret that made it impossible for us to go on? (*Faithful Women.*)

What if, after years of marriage, we won fifty million dollars in the lottery and got so out of whack that we nearly separated? (*Everything You Want*)

In each case, a character—*the* character—appeared. When I set her in motion, more and more and more characters came. Then I spent years imagining before-and-after moments in their lives that would help reveal the story.

There are before-and-after moments in the process of writing of each story, too. Images and ideas gather toward the moment you write the first word, moments of trial and error, and the moment when, finally, that most important character springs to life and sets off on a path.

There is nothing, *nothing*, more satisfying than that.

Up in Michigan

IT WAS AN UNSEASONABLY WARM MARCH DAY in northern Michigan. The sky was blue, the air crisp, warmed by the sun. The woods surrounding our getaway house were just starting to green up.

There was a strong breeze, so S. decided to set his favorite kite flying—a huge, handmade, silk rainbow kite. Once the kite was aloft, its vibrant color against the blue sky a welcome sight after a long gray winter, S. set a heavy rock on the kite-winder to hold it in place, and went to work cleaning out the shed and prepping the dirt bikes for summer.

Suddenly, a strong wind whipped up and yanked the kite-winder from under the rock. The kite took off, sailing across the meadow that faces our front door. S. hollered up at me for help. I threw on a jacket and ran outside to find S. already on his dirt bike, revving up the engine.

He nodded at the chainsaw he'd set on the picnic table, ready for its spring tune-up. "Grab that," he said.

I laughed, picked it up, and climbed onto the back of the bike. We bumped across the meadow onto a dirt road that leads into the woods. Pretty quickly, we spotted the kite caught high in a faraway tree. We hiked in to find it—a gargantuan oak.

S. grinned, powered up the chainsaw, and set it against the tree's massive trunk—a hopeless but amusing task. After several fruitless minutes, he set down the saw.

"Wait here," he said. "I'm going to get the gun."

I could not see how a gun would be useful here, but I said nothing. I sat on a log, basking in the sun, surveying the violets poking up through the soil, the green fringe emerging from the forest floor like hair. I breathed in the smell of spring.

When S. returned, he had a rifle and a box of shells. He had that look on his face I've seen countless time—the one that promises a zany adventure. His plan: to shoot the kite-winder and knock it loose from the tree. Shots rang out in the sharp air. S. hit the kite-winder a couple times, but it stayed put. Finally, after S. had used up most of the box of shells, he shot the kite-winder free. The kite was off again, over the trees.

S. and I tramped back out of the woods. He'd abandoned the dirt bike for his pick-up truck, so we clambered inside and headed for a clearing we knew where the kite might land. And sure enough, when we arrived at the clearing, there was the kite—now caught in a different, much smaller tree.

Using the chainsaw, S. cut down the tree. But instead of falling to the ground, it fell into a fork of high branches in the tree next to it, the kite still out of reach. So, S. used the chainsaw on that tree, too. This time, though, the chainsaw whined and sputtered out. S. pulled repeatedly on the starter, but it refused to revive. Undeterred, S. put the saw in the truck bed and extracted the axe he'd thrown in just in case. Then he took several whacks at the tree with the axe—to no avail.

By this time, we were both starving. So, we went back to the house for lunch.

"I'm getting that goddamn kite back," S. said.

After lunch, we climbed back into the truck and headed toward the clearing, each of us tossing out ideas for extracting the kite. But when we arrived, we found the kite already laid out for us in the middle of the grass. It was in perfect shape—not a rip in the silk, not a broken dowel. Even the kite-winder was intact, although chipped from the few bullets that had grazed it.

We were jubilant. We told the story again and again.

But it's not a story, really. It's an anecdote—a personal narrative with no real point other than to make people laugh. I realized I could *make* it a story, though, if I shaped it a little and worked in another layer of detail.

So, here goes—

We'd come to Michigan that weekend for some solitude after the death of S.'s father's. The two of them had been very close—partners in mischief, a two-person mutual admiration society.

When S. went to open the shed that morning, the first thing he saw, just outside the door, was the house key his dad—such a lovable klutz—had dropped in the deep snow a few months back and had been unable to find. Then, when S. opened the shed, he took in his dad's dirt bike parked side-by-side with his own, their skis hanging together from the same rack. He also spotted the rainbow kite, which his dad had given him the Christmas before—a gift more suited to a ten-year-old boy than an adult son.

Waiting in the woods while S. went back for the rifle, I remembered a snapshot of him sitting on the porch steps when he was four—so cute in his little striped shirt and brown oxford shoes. An earnest expression on his face. You couldn't tell from the photo, but he was watching a kite his dad had made and set flying during his lunch hour.

"Don't let it fly away, buddy," his dad had said as he left to go back to work at the local steel plant.

But that kite *did* fly away. Wind caught the kite-winder. S. chased it as it danced along the sidewalk, but then it went into the street—where he was not allowed to go. S. ran into the house, calling for his mom, but by the time they got back outside, the kite was gone.

S. burst into tears. He was inconsolable—so distraught that his mom had to call his dad at the plant. His dad immediately abandoned his post, drove to the dime store, bought a new kite, brought it home, put it together, and set it flying.

The fact of S.'s father's recent death, the details about their relationship, and the flashback to his childhood bring depth and meaning to what seems on the surface like a ridiculous quest. Suddenly, S.'s frantic search for the kite becomes a manifestation of grief. And the kite's return might represent a message from the cosmos telling S. that his dad had taught him all he needed to know to live his life. He would be able go on without him.

Or, it could be a message from S.'s father saying, "I'm still here."

So many first drafts of stories feel anecdotal: just one thing after another. *And then this happened, and then this, and then, and then, and then....* Reading them is like slaying the dragons that endlessly pop up in a video game with no purpose other than to trigger your finger on the joystick.

A real story reveals something unforgettable about its characters, about *life*, that stays with the reader after the events of the story fade.

"We Was Girls Together"

WINTER. 1974. MY AUNT AND I WERE chatting in the living room when I heard the whoosh of mail falling through the mail slot. I went to pick it up, rifled through the usual collection of bills and advertisements, still talking—until I came upon an envelope with familiar handwriting. It was a letter from my dearest college friend, E., normally a happy occasion for me. But a few days earlier, I had received a call from a police officer where she lived.

"Do you know her?" he'd asked. "How do you know her?" "When did you last see her?"

"Almost two years ago," I said. "Just before she moved away."

"Have you heard from her since?"

"Yes," I said. "I had a letter from her in the fall. But what is this about?"

E. was a member of a radical group suspected in the kidnapping of a young heiress, he had told me—headline news for the past several weeks.

"But E. wouldn't, she'd never—"

"She's a suspect," he repeated. "She disappeared with the rest of the group, and we're investigating every lead we can find. Your phone number was in the address book we found in her apartment." He had given me a phone number to call in case E. got in touch, and I had written it down Then I had sat abruptly on the floor, shocked and grief-stricken, certain that if what he'd said was true, if E. really was involved in the kidnapping, I'd never hear from her again.

Now there I was, her envelope in my hands, postmarked after the kidnapping had occurred.

"What is it?" my aunt asked. "Is something wrong?"

I showed her the letter and explained.

"You need to call the police *right now*," she said. "You don't know where those people are. They could hurt you."

E. wouldn't hurt me. Even as the kidnapping and its aftermath played out over the next 18 months, I never, *ever* doubted that. Nor did I doubt that, no matter what she'd done, I was still and always would be her friend. Wasn't that what friendship *meant*?

I remembered the two of us crowded with a bunch of other girls at the window of the sorority house in our nightgowns, laughing and yelling at the boys gathered below, some with girls' panties on their head, bras like necklaces or dangling from their fingers, begging for more.

And an unseasonably warm December day, wading the overflowing creek that ran through the campus, singing, eventually submerging ourselves in the pool that had formed in the yard of the fraternity house across the street from ours.

I remembered learning I was pregnant—an accident—and

dreading to share the news for fear of my sorority sisters' judgement or, worse, pity. How, amidst the other girls' horrified expressions, E. smiled and threw her arms around me. "Oh, a baby!" she said. "I can't wait."

To abandon her because of what she'd done, I'd have to pretend that these and so many other memories no longer mattered to me.

Still, when I opened E.'s letter that day and found evidence in it that clearly connected her to the kidnapping, I knew I could not remain silent. I didn't dare risk becoming an accessory to the crime, especially when the victim's life might be at stake. So, I called the number I'd been given, and soon found myself in the strange and unsettling position of being involved in an intense FBI investigation.

E.'s capture and imprisonment cracked my world open and challenged everything I thought I knew. If I could continue to be certain that, despite everything, E. was a good person, could the same be true of others who had committed such stunning acts of violence? Was *every* person who committed a criminal act similarly complex—their families and friends, like E.'s, remembering the good in them, broken-hearted by what they had done?

Under what set of circumstances might I do something terrible myself?

And there was this: Although I knew without a doubt that what E. had done was wrong, I deeply envied the passion that had brought her to the act. I wanted something I believed in that strongly, something of my own. I even knew what it was: writing.

What I wrote—what seemed *possible* to write then—were letters to E., in prison. Long letters, full of my life. This was my degree in creative writing, my own personal MFA: writing my life for this friend, laboring to bring it alive for her. An alternative existence. Another place for her to be.

And she wrote back—letters about how she spent her days in solitary confinement, the small courtyard where she wore a path running around and around the perimeter when she was allowed to go outdoors. What she was reading, thinking. What the women said, sharing confidences through the walls.

"We was girls together."

That's what Toni Morrison's character, Nel, says standing at the grave of her estranged friend, Sula, for the first time, years after her death. In the end, despite the pain caused by the sharply divergent paths their lives had taken, despite Nel's long refusal to acknowledge it, their girlhood bond could not be broken.

I've learned a lot of things from my friendship with E., but the most important thing I learned was that people are way more complicated than I had imagined. I thought I knew E. I *did* know her. I just didn't know *all* of her. I didn't even know all of myself. I never will. There is a mystery at the center of each one of us that can never be understood.

This is the basis for creating compelling characters in fiction.

When I opened my mind and heart to the paradox of being human, I understood that some act from a combination of beliefs formed by the experiences of their lives, some of which may be contradictory. They act from guilt and shame and sorrow. From hatred born of love. From love born of weakness and need.

Some act from a genuine desire to be good, but too often without realizing that what they think is good for someone they love might not be what that person wants or needs—or that it might even harm them. Some act from a desire to do harm, believing it is the only way to set right some horrific wrong. People act because they are influenced by people and ideas. They act because circumstances dictate that the time for ideas is over. They must decide in a split second whether to do something that will change their lives and the lives of those who love them forever.

In my view, a writer's greatest asset is insatiable curiosity about everything—but most importantly about the human condition. Writers who try to puzzle out what makes people do what they do in the real world know that it's impossible to create a fictional character from a set of traits. They recognize their characters in an image, in the rhythm of a name, in a blank space in a scene that needs another person in it—and invite them into the story.

People in fiction are like people in real life: They reveal themselves over time. Think of your first impression of someone you know well but haven't known forever. How did your sense of that person evolve as you got to know him better? What did his behavior under certain kinds of circumstances tell you about him? What did he do or say when he didn't know you were there that made you see something about him you hadn't seen before? What did someone else say to you about him that complicated your understanding of who he was?

Just as you trust your experiences with people to show you who they are, trust your characters to reveal themselves as they move through the scenes of your story—even if they upend what you thought you knew about them. Pay attention to the details of their existence. Consider the questions raised by their thoughts and actions in developing plots that hinge on who they are and worlds that reflect and reinforce their human qualities.

The Hitler Dollhouse

MY MOM WAS AN ENGLISH WAR BRIDE. If World War II had never happened, I would never have been born. Naturally, I've always been fascinated by how people lived through it. Traveling, I've seen countless traces of that war. The ruins of Coventry Cathedral in the West Midlands. The Memorial to the Martyrs of the Deportation, tucked underground behind Notre Dame in Paris. The concrete gun emplacements on the cliffs of Normandy. I've stood on Omaha Beach, where Allied troops landed on D-Day troops; toured Berchtesgaden, Hitler's secret bunker in the Alps; and stood in the barracks and by the ovens at Dachau, where more than forty thousand prisoners died.

I love standing in places where events that profoundly affected the world occurred. I like imagining how those places were then—even (maybe especially) when those things are painful to consider. I want to understand and remember—I feel it's my *responsibility* to understand and remember—the history of the world I live in.

From Dachau, for example, I remember the preserved set of barracks that showed the evolution of from what looked like rustic cabins, with one prisoner to each of the stacked bunks and space for a table and chairs, to nothing but long shelves where prisoners slept head to toe. I remember standing in the space between the barracks and the administrative building, where prisoners were forced to stand, sometimes for hours, freezing in the winter, broiling in the summer, as they waited to be counted or punished. I remember entering the gas chamber, never used, but—still. And the moment I looked at the opening of the oven where bodies were burned and realized each would have had to be placed in it—by a person, probably a Jew.

Somehow I thought it had been less personal than that.

On a more recent trip, wandering through the German Historical Museum in Berlin, I came upon an exhibit of toys from the WWII era, among them a dollhouse-sized kitchen. Its table, set with tiny plates and beer steins, delighted me. I loved the tiny red candle in its tiny silver candlestick, the tiny white bowl of fruit on the sideboard, the tiny cuckoo clock, the tiny sink and stove and vacuum cleaner. I marveled at the delicate lace curtains covering the windows.

Then I noticed the wallpaper: a repeating pattern of children in Hitler Youth uniforms on a pale green background. Some were lined up, saluting; some were in pairs, bearing the Nazi flag; some were sitting around a campfire; some were at work, pushing wheelbarrows filled with sheaves of wheat. I also noticed a miniature photograph of Hitler in a silver frame hanging between the two windows, and, beneath it, a tiny medallion with a swastika on it.

All I could think was—

Someone had the idea to manufacture this dollhouse.

Someone designed this wallpaper.

Someone shrunk the photograph of Hitler to dollhouse scale and framed it.

Someone made the mold for the Nazi medallion that hung on the wall.

And, perhaps worst of all, someone bought this dollhouse for their daughter.

Suddenly, I could see her: a blond, blue-eyed girl playing with the dollhouse on her bedroom floor, and with the perfect Aryan doll family that surely came with it. She moves the mother—blond and blue-eyed like herself—to set the meal on the table, calling out in a pretend-voice, *"Vater, kommen Sie. Es ist Zeit zu essen."* She picks up the father doll and sets him in one of the chairs. Then she makes the mother say, *"Kinder, du kommst auch."* Because, of course, there is a little blond boy doll and a little blond girl doll to join them at the table—no doubt dressed in tiny Hitler Youth uniforms, excited to tell their parents about the important work they did that day for the *Fuehrer*.

Who isn't horrified by the idea of Hitler Youth—the formal indoctrination of children in beliefs that resulted in untold cruelties and the deaths of more than eleven million innocent people, including six million Jews? I certainly am. But it's...I don't know. Abstract. Now, standing before this toy that was designed to corrupt a child's imagination, it became real. I saw just how a society could poison itself.

There are good details, and there are *great* details—like the Hitler dollhouse—that create what feels like a cataclysmic shift in your understanding of something you thought you knew. Details that beg to tell a story all their own—like the story of that little girl. Who was she? What happened to her? What does she have to teach me?

"Show, don't tell." This cardinal rule of fiction sounds simple, but it's not. It takes most students a long time to understand what the rule really means. "Oh," they think. "Details. I can do that." So, they write down every detail they can think of—so many that the story collapses under them. Worse, all too often they choose details without considering what crucial piece of information each one adds to the reader's understanding of the characters and of dilemma in which they find themselves. What a person is wearing might be important; or, it might not. The same is true for what kind of car they drive, how they furnish their apartment, what they have for dinner, what they carry in their backpacks, and so on.

Every story is a mystery; details are clues. Each clue should offer readers a piece of information that helps them come to their own conclusions about the characters, what's happening to them, and what it all means—just as they do with real people in real life. At times, they'll know more than the characters know themselves; this is one of reading's great pleasures.

Think of the Hitler dollhouse.

Imagine the little girl's family. Maybe her father was an S.S. officer responsible for countless atrocities. Her mother, blonde and beautiful, the perfect Aryan wife. Her brother and herself, enthusiastic members of Hitler Youth. Now imagine the girl grown and, like so many German children of the Third Reich, sickened and ashamed by what her country—not to mention what her own father, and what she herself—had done.

Imagine her coming upon that dollhouse in the attic of her family home when she's grown, memories of that time flooding back. For a moment, she is that little girl again, playing with the dollhouse she loved, talking in her dolls' voices about how Herr

Hitler is making a new world for only the best people; how, soon, the country will be rid of those dirty Jews.

And, back in her adult body, she finally, *truly* understands what no explanation, no book, no movie has ever been able to accomplish: The simple fact that the dollhouse had been manufactured for children like herself said everything anyone would ever need to know about how millions of good people were drawn into such horror.

Which is exactly what the dollhouse said to me.

Granted, details as fabulous as the Hitler dollhouse don't come along every day. Nonetheless, use it as a measure when you're trying to decide whether a detail you're considering is just a detail or a detail that's a clue.

"Telling details," we call them.

Pay attention. They're everywhere, in real life *and* in fiction.

"Y'all Had Enough Yardbird?"

WE WERE FINISHING UP DINNER WHEN STORYTELLER Dylan Pritchett stood, surveyed the group, and asked in his thick Virginia accent, "Y'all had enough yardbird?"

Anxious silence.

He grinned. "Y'all don't know what yardbird is?"

We didn't.

"Yardbird is slang for chicken in the Deep South," he told us. "So…y'all had enough yardbird?"

"Yes!" we said, laughing.

It was a great introduction to Pritchett's workshop on the most important aspect of storytelling: what people say and how they say it. In other words, dialogue.

"He was knee-walkin' drunk," a Southern friend said about someone at a party.

"I was gobsmacked," my English cousin said about something that amazed her.

"I am famous to lose myself," said an Italian woman to her American friends upon getting lost together in Rome.

"The only way you're going to talk me into running is to set the house on fire," said a woman to her very fit companion as I passed them on the street.

Maybe the difference between poets and fiction writers in their love of language is that poets fall in love with words themselves, while fiction writers delight in the way people use them. They are stopped short by bits of dialogue they hear as they go about their day-to-day lives.

Think of the blowsy waitress who calls everyone "honey." The prim aunt who says "sugar" instead of "shit." The teenager who uses "like" as others use might use a comma.

Every one of us—real or fictional—has a way of speaking that is instantly recognizable by those who know us. And it's more than just the words we use. Some people speak in short, even one-word, sentences. Others speak in long, rambling phrases. Some never finish a thought—bouncing from one idea to the next, trying to keep up with the rush of words in their head.

Different emotions elicit different words and rhythms. Think of how differently people speak to each other while making love, working out a conflict, or chatting with friends at dinner.

Think about unspoken dialogue: a shrug, a raised fist, a hug. Turning away.

Highlight the dialogue in a story you love—and the first thing you're likely to notice is that it doesn't occur in blocks, but is interspersed with action, gesture, and passages of narrative that provide clues about how the dialogue should be interpreted and create a rhythm that mirrors the mood of the conversation. Dialogue can also move the plot, pace, characterize, and supply details of setting.

Notice that good writers avoid using explanatory tags, like, He posited, articulated, lamented. They avoid using adjectives and adverbs to explain what the dialogue itself should convey: She said angrily: he said in furious voice. Except in extreme situations it's best to tag dialogue simply, with he said, she said, they said—or, perhaps, asked. These tags are invisible to readers, and work as a kind of punctuation as their eyes pause briefly over them, moving through the story.

Action or gesture can also be used as tags. "Okay." She raised her hands in surrender. "I give up!" Sometimes the speaker is obvious, and no tag is needed at all.

Dialogue, spoken or unspoken, carries clues about who your characters are and the situation they're in. I feel it inside as a kind of rhythm. Sometimes it flows easily to the page; more often, I spend a long time translating the rhythm of my characters' speech into words. I imagine it's something like creating lyrics for music that's already there. A wrong note in dialogue is like a wrong note in music. You really need to get it right.

"You get your goddamn Chinese-lookin' face out of here,"

I overheard one woman say to an Asian woman seconds before starting a knock-down, drag-out fight at a country dance. I was horrified. Yet, I couldn't help but appreciate how the language carried with it so much information about the woman who had spoken the words.

Which brings us to the very interesting question of when—and perhaps more importantly when *not*—to use "offensive" language in a story. In 1996, scanning the list of the "100 Most Banned Books of the Year" in my recent *Authors Guild Bulletin*, I came upon my own book, *Wish You Were Here*. I was ecstatic! Seriously. I was in great company.

The book had been banned because it contained references to sexual activity among adolescents. What the book *didn't* contain was the "F" word. My publisher had been worried that including it might affect the book's sales and its reviews in the YA market, so I replaced each instance of *fuck* with *screw*.

I instantly regretted this. Worse, it seemed like each time I visited a school to talk about the book, some kid would say that he didn't think Brady, one of the book's main characters, would say "screw" instead of "the F word."

Embarrassed, all I could say was, "You're right."

In 2009, a different publisher bought the rights to *Wish You Were Here*. I told my new editor that I regretted having stripped the *fucks* out from the book's first edition. "Put them back in!" he said. So, I did—with pleasure. I especially liked the effect on Brady's monologue at the graveside of a classmate, near the end of the book:

"I have a theory about this," he says, pompous as a teacher. "Take

Jim Morrison, man, the ultimate fuckup, you think. I know this guy who went to his grave in Paris. It's a mecca for fuckups, he said. Every fuckup in the world wants to go to Jim's grave. But I say Morrison was an amateur. He got to twenty-seven. Big deal. My theory is you haven't really fucked up until there's no way you can possibly redeem yourself...Morrison was twenty-seven, Jax. A baby. Joplin, Hendrix. Babies. Mama Cass, stoned, choking on a goddam ham sandwich. Belushi, even. Babies, all of them. But let's talk about Elvis! Elvis made it to forty-two, a fat, pill-popping slob. A spoiled brat. 'Bring me girls! Bring me cheeseburgers!' This guy made fucking up an art form. And the beauty of it is, he didn't even know he was fucking up. He didn't even try. It came natural to him. Yeah, King Fuckup...You know what we ought to do, Jax? We ought to go [to Graceland]."

How could I ever have convinced myself that *screw* would suffice?

But authentic dialogue in a story is only part of a story's voice. One year I had a football player in my creative-writing class—a smart, funny kid who loved to read. The first story he wrote was about an orphaned child who longed for a family. It was set in London. This kid had never been to London, so the details of place were all wrong. And, he had attempted to write a cockney dialect, which—when I read it in the privacy of my office—made me laugh out loud.

I am always honest with students. So, when I met with this boy to discuss his story, I told him why it didn't work. "It's not that you're not allowed to write from the point of view of a person unlike yourself or about a place you're unfamiliar with," I said. "It's that if you choose to do that, you have to do your research to make sure you get that person and that place *right*."

I suggested that this time around, it might be a good idea to stick closer to home. "What's your favorite book?" I asked, thinking that would help me direct him to more manageable material.

"*Little House on the Prairie*," he said. "Man, I love that book!"

"Oh, my gosh," I said. "That was my favorite book as a kid, too!"

Here we were—a bookish white woman in her forties and a seventeen-year-old African American football player—and a big chunk of our material was exactly the same: longing for the perfect family. My job was to help him recognize that material as his and prepare him for the moment when he was good enough to make a leap beyond the world and people he knew.

In these days of escalating concerns about political correctness, though, there is considerable controversy surrounding the question of what writers are allowed to imagine. Recently, I wrote a YA novel whose main character is a gay boy. But I couldn't sell it. My exasperated agent explained that several editors had rejected it because they were looking for "authentic" voices—and as a straight woman, I didn't qualify. Indeed, some editors seemed to view the fact that I had written the book at all as some type of transgression. I sensed that they would have thought the same thing if the character had been African American, Latinx, Muslim, trans, overweight, a victim of rape or abuse, and so on.

Should voices be authentic? Yes. Absolutely. But it is absurd to limit fiction writers to creating characters only like themselves. Think about it: If you apply this rule to crime fiction, only people who had committed a crime would be qualified to write it. Only teenagers could write YA novels. And you could forget about historical fiction. After all, if the writer wasn't alive during the period in question, how could they ever guess what it might have been like to live through it? Or, try applying this rule to past works. You'd have to pull Eudora Welty's "A Worn Path," Kazuo Ishiguro's *The Remains of the Day*, and Edith Wharton's *Ethan Frome* from bookstores and library shelves—not to mention Gustave Flaubert's *Madame Bovary* and Willa Cather's *Death Comes to the Archbishop*.

I don't believe there's anything a writer should be forbidden to imagine. Imagining a character completely unlike you in a world completely unlike your own often enables you to tackle one of your life questions from a slant. And ironically, this type of character is often more powerful than one that is more like you. This is because when you create them, you must depend on your observations about what they do and say, and on your imagination to determine whether those observations provide clues to meaning and possibility. In contrast, when you write a character like yourself, you unconsciously depend on what you know, making it difficult to make the necessary lift from fact to fiction.

Imagination is at the root of every good story. Creating characters, living in the worlds and heads of people unlike yourself, is what writing fiction *is*. Besides, *everybody* but you is not you—even your twin sister. If you were to limit yourself to writing characters based only on your own personal experiences, you'd quickly run out of story ideas—and the art of fiction would suffer from it.

Dr. Beat and the Archangels

I HAD A WONDERFUL, GENEROUS MENTOR—AN OLDER writer named V. She often told a story about a writing retreat she'd taken to Italy with some friends that had gone bad. First there was confusion about money. Then there was a woman who picked up a man and brought him back to their *pensione* in Florence. A daffy poet in the group got crazier and crazier as the trip went on. The woman who organized the retreat had a meltdown because the others didn't seem appropriately grateful. V. played it as a comedy of errors, which never failed to make me laugh.

V. named me her literary executor. So, when she died, it fell to me to sort through the literary work she'd left behind—including her journals. In them I found an account of the trip and its aftermath that revealed it hadn't been funny at all. In fact, V.'s time in Italy had shaken her confidence both as a person and a writer and created rifts among the group that were never mended. V. had looked forward to the trip—her first real independent excursion abroad—with such anticipation; it hurt my heart to discover what a disaster it had truly been. Indeed, V. never really traveled independently again.

Reading about V.'s experience abroad planted the seed of a novel in my mind. Some years later, I received a grant to spend a month in Italy with three other writers to do research for it. We chose a tiny Umbrian hill town called Montone as our destination. This decision was based on a single photograph sent by the landlord of one of the flats we were considering renting. It depicted the dark tip of a mountain floating like an iceberg above an ocean of fluffy white clouds, "our" medieval village perched on top, backed by a cobalt-blue sky.

Our month in Montone was rich in outings to places we'd all longed to see, intimate moments sharing joys and heartbreaks, delicious conversations about writing and books, and lots of laughter. There were small tensions, of course, but nothing like V. had experienced on her retreat. Truthfully, I had such a good time that I forgot about V. altogether.

I existed in a constant state of wonder. How could I not? The hills rolled out around me, villages on top like little hats. Flowers everywhere—petunias cascading from balconies and window boxes; wisteria, jasmine, lavender; geraniums and blue hydrangeas in clay pots beside our door. Ghostly fresco fragments on church walls like puzzle pieces—patches of landscape, faces, a hand, a boot, a scepter. One morning we woke to a dense fog—and to clouds in our kitchen.

As I neared the end of my time in Montone, I hadn't written one single word of that novel. My journal entry from our last day there says:

I woke up thinking about what I wanted, what I thought this experience would be, what it is. I wanted time and space to work. A beautiful, stimulating place to work in. I could kill two birds with one stone, I thought: travel and write—collecting all the fabulous details I'd need for the novel along the way. I liked the discipline of knowing that I'd been given money—entrusted with money—to write a novel. Therefore, I thought, I must write that novel. I am responsible to do that. I would come to Italy and work, work, work on that novel. I would use Italy, build that novel from what I saw and did here...[It would be] time away from the drudge and

distraction of daily life to concentrate on the pure thing: writing, art. But I have forgotten to use this time to write, forgotten to browbeat myself to write. I'm like the girl in E. M. Forster's Room with a View: *"…the pernicious charm of Italy worked on her, and instead of acquiring information, she began to be happy."*
And I was.

Over the past twenty years, I've tried and failed to write that novel so many times, I've lost count. But giving up on a novel feels a lot like giving up on a child, so I'm guessing I'll keep trying. If I live long enough, I'll make it work.

I will.

Either way, I wouldn't trade that month in Montone for anything. Nor would I trade the surprising lesson I learned there: that it's important to be a disciplined writer, but it's also important to know when to ignore the voice in your head that tells you to stay focused, miss nothing, and write down every little detail and just *live*—trusting that everything you need will be there when it's time to turn that moment you are living into words.

When I returned home from Montone, I found myself frustrated trying to explain to my family and friends what my time there had been like, and by trying to write about the experience. Finally, months later, I remembered Chekhov's decree: "Don't tell me the moon is shining. Show me the glint of light on broken glass." *Duh,* I thought. *Show, don't tell. It's Fiction 101.* So, I sat down at my computer, and suddenly Montone flowed through my fingers onto the page:

> *In Montone, all streets lead to the piazza, and on this warm summer evening we drift down Via Roma for the village dance.*

Dr. Beat and the Archangels are scheduled to play at 9:00, but it's Italy. Nobody seems to notice that the church bells toll 9:00, 9:30, 9:45, and the boys in the band are still fooling around, setting up on the wide stoop in front of the shop where, afternoons, the ladies of the town sit with their needlework, gossiping. The townspeople are drinking wine, laughing, flirting at the café tables. Children careen around the piazza, screaming; old men perch, smoking, on a low wall near the Café Aries. There is the hiss of the espresso machines from the cafés, the clink of cups and saucers, the smell of jasmine. Night falls, indigo blue, scalloped by red roof tiles.

There I am: a woman of a certain age cut loose from the pleasures and distractions of my real life, living for a little while in the novel I want to write. Often, I feel lost in time. I fall asleep to footsteps on stone, ringing anvils, the yowl of a cat: ancient sounds. Mornings, I throw open the shutters of my window and watch the swallows swooping and shrieking, framed in the foreground of a Renaissance landscape. One day, in Monterchi, I stood before Piero della Francesca's "Madonna del Parto" and saw in the face of the presenting angels my favorite waitress at the Café Erba Luna.

A few evenings ago, I watched the sun set from the walled garden outside the cloisters at San Francesco. It was orange, like fire. It hung suspended just above a single mountain peak for a long time, floating in wisps of cloud, then disappeared quite suddenly, leaving streaks of pale orange on the sky. That night I waited for music, too. Inside the cloisters, chrome and white director chairs were set in angled rows on the stone floor. There were chairs for the musicians in one corner, silver music stands, a harpsichord. Potted plants on the floor, on the low wall. A worn Persian rug in the place where the director would stand. La musica da camera, *the program promised. Chamber music: music of the room.*

The musicians entered, dressed formally in black and white, and it began. I loved looking at them: watching their hands on the bows. I loved the way the burnished red cello glowed in the lamplight cast from the corner of the arched colonnade, the way the sheet music was held in place with plastic clothespins on the silver stands. I loved the sheet music itself, just black lines on white paper; yet a language in its own right, translated into Elgar's Serenata. Vivaldi's Le Quattro Stagioni.

Now the twang of an electric guitar brings me back to the piazza. Tonight.

"Ciao," Dr. Beat hollers to the crowd in the piazza.

And in this Umbrian hill town that legend says sheltered Dante in his exile more than six hundred years ago, he and the Archangels begin to play. The Rolling Stones, "Paint It Black."

Then "Wipeout," "Louie Louie," "A Hard Day's Night."

Everyone is dancing. The mayor, the gossiping ladies, the greengrocer and his wife. Federico, the owner of the Café Erba Luna, leaves the gelato counter to dance with the Piero waitress, Stephanie. Little girls run and scream, tug at the shirt tails of the teenage boys until they lift them up and dance with them on their shoulders. Friendly Sylvio wheels among them all, marvelous turquoise socks peeking from beneath his trousers.

I have never been so truly happy. The piazza is such a lovely place to be, with its blue-tiled tables and striped awnings. Its peeling pink-faced buildings, geraniums trailing over wrought iron balconies. Church bells ring from the bell tower above this open box of night.

When Dr. Beat and the Archangels play the opening riff of "I Can't Get No Satisfaction," I'm a senior in high school, lonely, miserable, trapped, singing along with the car radio. I'm a sweaty disheveled college student, shouting out the words at a fraternity party. A young mother, dancing with my husband and daughters in a tacky little country bar. A writer, a traveler, a woman of a certain age—not young.

Cigarette smoke, trellised roses, I scribble. Breeze, iron lanterns, shadows. But the pernicious charm of Italy works on me, and I put down my notebook and dance.

Drawing Boxes

"EVERYTHING FITS IN A BOX," MY DRAWING teacher said on the first day of class. "If you can draw a box, you can draw anything."

Which turned out to be a lot harder than you might think.

Still, I loved getting lost in the lines and angles, laboring to get one box right, then the one next to it, and the one behind. I had to keep remembering that I was drawing a particular box, the one in front of me—right now. If I moved, the composition changed, and the lines I drew no longer matched up to the box I thought I was drawing.

It reminded me of what happens if you hang one strip of wallpaper slightly out of plumb. At first it seems like no big deal, but when you get to where the wallpaper meets where you started you find you've created a very unfortunate slant.

Or when you start writing a story and go so randomly from one character's head to another's that the story loses focus. Even though you're still working with exactly the same set of circumstances, the story you're writing becomes completely different.

Perspective, or point of view, establishes the world of a story and dictates its limitations. If you choose to tell a story from one character's point of view, you have to keep seeing the world of the story through that character's eyes. If, suddenly, you start looking at what's happening through a different character's eyes, the whole world shifts—and the effect is as jarring as a wrong angle in a drawing.

Telling a story from multiple points of view is like crossing a stream on stepping stones. You move from one character to the next throughout the story, telling what they see and know from where they stand. Generally, it's good to keep the points of view in some balance. They don't have to be used equally, but if you get to the end and find you've used one or several points of view considerably fewer times than the others, consider whether what those point of view characters know is necessary or might be told by someone else.

You can tell a story from the omniscient point of view, too—dipping in and out of characters' heads as if you are God. But it's a tricky thing to do well. Same for stories told in the second person and the collective "we."

As for which point of view to use? Go with your instinct. More often than not, point of view comes with the story. If that doesn't happen, experiment until you get it right. Just remember, changing the point of view changes the whole story. Also remember that, as a drawing gets out of whack if the artist shifts position, a story get out of whack if the writers permit characters to know things it would be impossible for them to know.

Making a story works depends on telling it from where each character stands—more specifically, on what they see and feel and know from where they stand. Numerous characters can stand in the same place but not it in the same way. But what, exactly, does that mean?

Imagine being born with a clear lens, with which—for an instant—you see the world as it really is. But beginning with your very first breath, even your smallest, seemingly insignificant experience grinds the lens so that, increasingly, the world becomes a reflection of what those experiences condition you to see and feel.

Think about a something that happened recently. It can be anything—a trip to the park, a day at the office, coffee with a friend. Then close your eyes. Bring the scene to your mind's eye. See. Smell. Taste. Touch. Listen. Jot down everything your senses told you, then free-write the scene.

Next, write about how the scene made you feel.

Now write about what you can't know because of where you stood in the scene. Consider what others in the scene could know from where they stood, and how that might be different—might even contradict—what you saw from your position.

Think about what you noticed that others who shared the experience are likely to have missed. Then think about the opposite: what others might have seen that you likely overlooked. Finally, think about how the scene affected you emotionally, and how it might have affected others who were there.

Try this, too: Talk with siblings or close friends about a shared experience from a while back, one you feel strongly about. But be prepared for arguments because there's a good chance they'll disagree about when and how it happened, who was there, how it turned out, what it meant. And nobody will be lying. What actually happened lies somewhere in the mix of all of those memories, impossible to know. It's why point of view is so difficult, why getting it right is crucial to making a story work.

Writers must know what their characters can see and hear from where they stand and how that changes as their line of vision changes, moving through the story. They must also know their characters well enough to know what they would and wouldn't *notice* from where they stand, based on how those imaginary lenses are ground. What do they notice instantly, surveying a scene? What do they look for? What do they miss or ignore because of who they are? Would they see the scene in broad terms, or in minute detail? What would they conclude about what's happening because of the way the world shaped them? How do the things they notice make them feel? What memories to they trigger?

Attending an auto race with S. not long ago, I noticed the light falling on a stack of fat black tires, the vibrant colors of the cars, billboards, fans in baseball caps that declared allegiance to drivers, teams, products, countries, and the racing series itself. I noticed drivers in their fireproof suits and cool slipper-like driving shoes, mechanics in their team shirts. The safety crew in their fireproof suits and yellow helmets made me think of the Fisher Price figures my daughters used to play with.

S., a race fan since childhood, noticed the sound of the engines being tuned up, the fact that the wrap on one driver's car had been changed since the last race due to a sponsorship issue. He saw a mechanic on his knees, working on a car with its front off, and knew from that detail that the radio system was malfunctioning. He recognized retired drivers, media personalities who covered racing. Remembered attending auto races with his dad when he was a kid.

The stories we told about our day at the race were completely different.

Flannery O'Connor said, "Point of view will run you crazy."

It will probably run you crazy, too.

When that happens, breathe. Look at the light where you are. Notice where it falls, what it illuminates, what remains in shadow.

Move. See how it changes.

Then turn back to your work. Go on.

A Day in the Life

THE POET BORGES IS SAID TO HAVE observed, "Time is the only problem." This seems right to me—in life and in fiction. Set out to write down every single thing that happened to you in a day, and you will soon find yourself mired in mostly irrelevant detail. If you write down every single thing that happens to your characters from the beginning of a story to its end, the same thing will occur.

Time is fluid. It's fickle. Confounding. It's the problem at the heart of every story because it dictates the story's flow—how it is structured and told. Eudora Welty put it this way: "The events in our lives happen in a sequence in time, but in their significance to ourselves they find their own order, a timetable not necessarily—

perhaps not possibly—chronological. Time as we know it subjectively is often the chronology that stories and novels follow: it is the continuous thread of revelation."

To cut through the swirl of time surrounding the story you want to write, think of the main character's life progressing predictably, day-by-day, as fixed action, and something that disrupts that daily rhythm as moving action. The latter might be a death, an injury, a new kid in school, the revelation of a secret—anything that sets a series of events in motion. The moving action creates a problem (the beginning) that the characters wrestle with (the middle) until it is resolved (the end.) The arc made from the moving action to its resolution is the time frame of the story—its "now."

You can diagram this. First, draw a line that represents the main character's life, and mark the moment the moving action occurs with an X. Next, draw X's to mark scenes along the continuum of now to the point of resolution. Drawing a half circle above those points will give you the arc and flow of the story. If your book contains flashbacks, indicate them with arrows pointing down beneath the now, their length indicating how far back in time they go. And, by the way, flashbacks are used when—and only when—they provide crucial information about what's happening in the novel's present.

A trick I learned in a workshop with former *Atlantic* editor Michael Curtis offers another way to identify your story's now, or its focus. Finish this sentence using as much detail as you can: "This is a story about what happened when..."

The finished sentence doesn't have to be beautiful; it just has to say clearly what the story is about. When you get it right, you'll have created a standard against which to judge whether characters, scenes, ideas, and plot twists in your story actually belong there. Anything that doesn't bring clarity, depth, or complexity to the focus defined by your sentence should be abandoned. Flashbacks exist only to give the reader background information essential to understanding what's happening in the now.

Notice that the sentence doesn't say, "This a story about...," but rather, "This is a story *about what happened...*" *About* leads to abstractions and ideas. *What happened* leads to a progression of moments and scenes grounded in time.

There's a good chance you won't actually be able to complete this sentence when you first start working on your story, or that you'll complete it only to find that it changes as the story evolves. You might even write several drafts of the story before getting it down right. But the sentence and the visual structure it creates in your mind's eye help keep you on track—a reminder that everything in the story must directly relate to *what happened when*.

This strategy for identifying a story's boundaries is wonderfully simple—but not easy. Stories get away from us. They surprise us—often becoming something we had no idea we were going to write. Fixed and moving action in the structure may move as a story evolves; the flashbacks may change.

What person in the world goes through life in a straight line?" Gail Godwin asked an interviewer. "I'm sure as you drove up this driveway, you were not totally in the present moment: You were all over your life, maybe in your dreams as well. I think that most people, whether aware of it or not, are never in one place or time. We have this idea of linear time imposed on us... [But] if you start looking at it, it's all here and now."

Discovering how time works in your story is not the only problem. But when the continuous thread of revelation finally reveals itself and you free yourself and your story from linear time, you'll have created the order you need to deal with the rest of the story's problems one-by-one.

Jump

Take a Deep Breath

IN HER REAL LIFE, N. IS A criminal defense attorney in New York City. But for two weeks every summer, she is a writer. "I don't want to write a novel," she said when she began attending Art Workshop International, in Assisi. "I just want to write."

N. said she could only write from prompts. So, her instructor gave her prompts:

Write a scene with flowers in it.

Write a scene that takes place in a hotel.

Write a scene with a monkey in it.

Write a dialogue in which two characters disagree.

As N. wrote, a set of characters began to emerge. They were connected to each other by legal issues surrounding a fictional Mexican man in prison on drug charges. Pages piled up.

"Not pages of a novel," N. insisted—although they sure seemed like pages of a novel to the rest of us.

Art Workshop International instructors and students fall in love with Assisi and return again and again. A walk through the town takes you up and down narrow winding medieval streets warmed by the sun, past ancient fountains, small shrines tucked into niches, faded frescos above ordinary houses. You might see the penitent, a man dressed in sack cloth, carrying a staff, who walks to the basilica on his knees each morning. You might see cats on a wide ledge feasting on open tins of cat food brought by an old lady in black who stands guard, glowering at tourists. A steep shopping street offers St. Francis souvenirs, gelato, ceramics, clothing, pastries, wine, olive oil, and meringue as big as a baby's head.

N. only occasionally ventured out of the Hotel Giotto to explore these wonders. Mostly she wrote.

When it was time to return to her jam-packed life in New York, she swore she was going to find time to write over the next year—but she never did. Around year five, N. finally—reluctantly—admitted that she was writing a novel. She began to depend less on prompts. Each piece she wrote started to lead naturally to the next piece that needed to be written. But at the end of each workshop, she went back to New York, once again leaving us all to wonder for a whole year what would happen next.

Despite the annual abandonment of her characters, N. has made huge leaps in thinking about how novels work. Near the end of her last workshop, she and I made a spreadsheet of all the bits and pieces she'd written. First, we identified parts of the story—a prologue, negotiations with a prisoner, the prisoner in jail, the trip to Mexico, the plight of one character who'd been left behind. Then we put each section in chronological order, noting chapter divisions as we went. N. began to see the gaps that would require new chapters.

The novel is alive and humming. "I'm going to work on it at home this year," N. said the day we left. "I mean it. I really am."

Will she? I don't know.

But I *do* know that eventually she will finish that novel, and it will be good.

All of this is to say that there's no one way to begin writing a story.

Some writers make a plot outline before writing the first word. Some create extensive character profiles. But neither of these activities counts as actually *beginning*. And there's a real danger of losing interest in the story once you've figured everything out. You can talk a story to death in the same way. (And trust me: There is *nothing* more boring than listening to a writer's blow-by-blow account of a story he *intends* to write.) Thinking obsessively about how to begin writing a story just creates a loop of possibility, frustration, and doubt in your mind that makes beginning it seem impossible.

Good stories evolve. They surprise you. A writer's best-conceived plots can change in an instant when a character does something that alters everything the writer thought she knew, or if a character the writer hadn't imagined appears. This doesn't mean you shouldn't make an outline if you find it helpful. Just be prepared to set it aside after you begin writing the story if it takes an unexpected turn that makes better sense.

Try writing off the top of your head until suddenly—who

knows why?—you write a sentence that opens a path into the story. Or write a scene—any scene—without worrying where or even whether it fits in the bigger picture. Write the ending and work backward to see where the story begins. Imagine a photograph of your characters and free-write about what's going on outside the frame. Write nothing but a series of lines of dialogue; then figure out who's saying what, why they're saying it, and what triggered the dialogue in the first place. At the top of a page, write, "Dear [Main Character], Would you please tell me where your story begins?" Let her answer. Or, like N., start with a prompt and see who shows up.

Sometimes the very first line of a novel that comes to you stays in place as the novel's beginning. One day, during the build-up to the war in Iraq—which coincided closely with the death of my sister—I spent a day roaming the campus of Indiana University. Grieving both for my sister and for how our country had clearly forgotten the lessons of Vietnam, I revisited places that had been important to me during my time there in the mid-1960s, reminiscing—wondering if the world and my own smaller realm within it would ever be set right.

That evening, I sat down and wrote this sentence: "Nora Quillen sat on a bench in People's Park, considering what was lost." I had no idea who Nora Quillen was or what she'd lost. But that sentence was so compelling that I followed it into what eventually became my novel, *An American Tune*, about a woman whose political acts during the Vietnam era finally catch up with her. I still don't understand exactly what triggered what remained the first line of that novel I had no idea I was going to write.

Writers tinker endlessly with story beginnings—those crucial first words designed to pull a reader in. But beginning to write a story and a story beginning are completely different things. Those first words and pages you write might or might not be the beginning of your finished story. In fact, it's not uncommon to complete the entire draft of a story or novel before you see where it should start. So, worry about the actual beginning of your story later.

Right now, take a deep breath.

Take another.

Jump.

Then What?

This is my earliest memory. Night. The moon is round and white, framed in my bedroom window. Its light makes a shadow of the big tree on the wall above me. My swing hangs from the highest branch, motionless now. But it's mine, safe in my room with me. All my things are with me. My doll, my book, my blanket. My shoes are on the dresser. They shine, white as the moon. I can smell the fresh polish on them. I drift off to sleep with one thumb in my mouth and the other rubbing the satin ribbon of my blanket—

My novel *Faithful Women* begins with this first memory of my friend, P., who was raised by her mother and two aunts while her father and uncles were away during World War II. She was the center of their universe. To her, they comprised one perfect mother, uniquely equipped to meet her every need.

"He's too big," P. said, at three years old, when her father returned.

Soon enough, P. came to adore him. But I was transfixed by the idea of a child cherished by these lonely sisters, by the shock of her large, loud father appearing and her aunts disappearing to live with their own large, loud men.

My fiction-mind wouldn't let it go. What if P. had felt more in tune with one of those aunts than with her own mother? What if P.'s mother—just eighteen years old when P. was born—had gone to work in a factory, as so many women did then, and had enjoyed that freedom and independence? What if P.'s mother and father fought about this when he returned from the war? What if, on a night out, having had too much to drink, P.'s mother stormed from the restaurant and was killed by an oncoming car? What if P.'s father had fallen in love with an English woman while stationed in London but, determined to honor his marriage, had abandoned her and returned home after the war? What if, freed by his wife's death, P.'s father returned to London to marry that woman? What if P., left with the aunt she loved while her father was gone, resented her new stepmother—not to mention her three baby stepsisters, who were born in quick succession over the next few years. What if P. couldn't understand why she couldn't just live with her beloved aunt forever?

I meant to write one of those juicy family sagas—the events that occurred during the war and its aftermath reverberating down through the generations that followed. But after I finished the first section—the part loosely based on P. and her three mothers—P. and I took a trip to Holland and I fell in love with the Dutch painter Johannes Vermeer. In a flash I decided my fictional unhappy daughter would be an art conservator who specialized in

17th-century Dutch art. (This provided me with an excuse to learn more about Vermeer and his world.) I'd tell the story of how she flees the Midwest for New York, where she devotes herself to her work, determined to avoid emotional entanglements. Then she's called to repair a slashed Vermeer in London's National Gallery. There, she comes face to face with her English stepmother's wartime experience and resolves the bitterness and resentment she feels toward her.

The next year, P. and I spent a month in England. Both of us set out on separate adventures each morning and met for dinner to talk about all we'd discovered. A Latin teacher, P. had received a grant to study Roman Britain, and spent her days exploring Roman ruins in London and sites beyond.

I visited the Imperial War Museum and Churchill's War Room. I toured my mom's old neighborhood in the city's East End, where you could still see remnants of bombed-out buildings. I imagined the shriek of sirens, the roar of bombers in the dark sky. I found the pub in Newmarket, where my parents met and fell in love, and where I talked to a woman who'd been a girl during the war and remembered the GI's coming into town on trucks from the army base where my dad had been stationed. I listened to my older English relatives tell stories about their experiences during the war.

With vague directions from my mom, I found the country estate that had been requisitioned to billet members of the Women's Royal Air Force during the war—including my mom. When I told the house's current occupant that she'd been stationed there, he invited me to explore the grounds. I imagined the Quonset huts that had once stood in what was now a peaceful meadow behind the house. There was an ancient chestnut tree, a small medieval chapel, a lovely little pond. The man told me there had been a rack of communal bicycles that the women had ridden to and from their shifts at the control center in a barn a mile or so away—and into town, as my mom had done, on the night she met my father.

I toured the conservation lab in the National Gallery so I could accurately place my main character there, and I returned numerous times to the gallery that housed the Vermeer I'd chosen to be slashed. I visited the Vermeers in other museums, too—studying the rich interiors surrounding the serene, timeless women he painted. Musical instruments, framed maps, richly patterned Turkish rugs. Black-and-white marble floors, velvet-curtained sleeping cabinets. Pearls, goblets, letters, freshly baked bread. Every small detail a clue to who he was and how he saw the world he lived in.

Occasionally, I accompanied P. to Roman sites. I became fascinated by the evidence of life two thousand years ago. One day my English cousin took us to Silchester, once the site of the Roman town Calleva Atrebatum. After he parked the car in the churchyard, we walked under a great gnarled yew tree and through a little cemetery with crumbling gravestones onto a rutted path that was knee-high with weeds, laced with stinging nettles, and buzzing with insects. We followed it along the edge of a cultivated field, then up the mound of earthworks to the Roman wall, the only part of the ancient town still visible. We walked a ways along the top—as wide as a city sidewalk.

After a picnic lunch, we walked down to a small museum that held artifacts from excavations that had begun in the 19th century. Near the end of the exhibit, my cousin directed our attention to a pattern of crisscrossing yellowish lines on an aerial photograph of the field we'd just walked past.

"The lines are the grid of the Roman streets below," he told us.

I was, as the British say, gobsmacked—just as he knew I would be.

Soon after I got home, I sat down to work on *Faithful Women*. Instead, on impulse, I typed the childhood memory P had shared with me long ago, and wrote—I didn't even *know* what.

A character appeared that I hadn't imagined in the original idea for the novel: a British archaeologist, an expert in Roman Britain, a man carrying his own bitterness about the war. He takes my character, named Evie, to Silchester, a few weeks after she arrives in London. She's undone by her attraction to him—by his passion for history, and by his frankness about life. She finds herself talking about things she's never talked about to anyone.

Life is like archaeology, he tells her. *You must know your past to know yourself. You must suffer the exhaustion, the filth, the tedium of digging. You must be patient. Brave. You must learn to cherish what you find, even if it's not what you hoped for, even if it renders meaningless all you found before.*

She doesn't want to believe it.

Toward the end of the scene, he describes the photograph I saw the day P. and I visited Silchester.

"Buried, gone—" he says of the Roman town. *"We English are so sensible, you know. We've worked the site. Museums hold what we've found here, safe, and now the rich farmland is put back into proper use. But in the autumn the town reasserts itself. Evie, if you could see it from the air!*

"The wheat and barley can't root so deeply where the gravel streets were, or above the remains of the flint walls. As the season changes and the plants receive less moisture, those above the streets and walls grow poorly. They're shorter than the others, unhealthy. Ripening, they reach maturity and turn yellow sooner than the other plants. From the air, you can see the grid of Roman streets in them—yellow lines on a green field. In a very dry season, you can even see the narrower lines of walls and houses."

She understands that he's saying the past is present in her life, too, and she's afraid.

Whoa, I thought. Who knew the book was going to be about that?

I'd been blown away by Silchester's visual metaphor of the past. But I hadn't really thought of it since the day of the outing—and it certainly hadn't occurred to me that my experience there would have anything to do with the novel I was writing. Roman Britain was P.'s area of interest, not mine! Yet, unbeknownst to me, my writer-brain had added Roman Britain to the mix of material sloshing around in my head—and out came the scene I'd just written.

Somehow, I knew the scene was crucial—and that it spoke to the difficult relationship I had with my own English mother. Maybe *I* was the one who was afraid. In any case, it took me the better part of a year to accept the fact that the scene was trying to tell me I needed to write a whole different book.

So, I did, clueless at many points along the way.

It's happened to me more than once: the appearance of a character so compelling and insistent that the book I thought I was writing metamorphosed beneath my typing fingers into something entirely new. It's happened to many other writers I've spoken with, too. There's no logical explanation for why it happens—little or no explanation for any part of the creative process, for that matter.

Attempting to describe what it feels like to write a novel in *Novel Ideas: Contemporary Novelists Share the Creative Process*, I wrote:

Writing a novel feels like this to me: You have seen or felt or dreamed something that you can't name, but that you know you can't live without. You set out on a journey to find it. There is no map; no one has ever been to this place. You barely know the people you are traveling with—your characters—but you know they are the only people who know the way. You watch them, listen to them. You follow along, putting down the words to mark the path they make. It is a long journey, with many wrong turns and surprises. Every day, or as often as you can, you go to the world of the novel. Months pass. Sometimes years.

Your journey through this world becomes an alternate reality. The people you "see" there every day are as real and confounding as your own family. You live with these characters, worry about them at unlikely moments. You are amazed, sometimes, at the way all kind of things work their way into the story: personal experiences, newspaper stories you read, stories friends and family tell in passing, memories, ideas that delight you. The occasional glimpse of something beautiful, funny, or sad that you can't forget. A passion for some person, place, or thing that you feel compelled to preserve—or that, perhaps, your life in the real world can't accommodate.

Sometimes, you have to stop and do research; sometimes, you have to stop and get a clear picture of what's actually on the page as opposed to what's in your head. Sometimes, like a recalcitrant child, the book just stops and you have to trick and tease it into moving forward. The novel won't be all you hoped it would be, but you keep on anyway. To abandon it now would be unthinkable, like walking away from your own imperfect life.

This process of trial and error can take a year, two years, five years—twenty.

Eventually, finally, it is done. For a few days you feel wonderful, free. You attend to business, clean your house, rake your yard, change the oil in your car, read, watch movies, spend a day at the beach. You actually pay attention when someone is talking to you. Then you begin to miss where the novel took you, the people in it, what it was. You feel anxious. There's nothing to organize your life around. What are you going to do?

Have you written every single thing you know?

Yes, if you were doing it right.

But pretty soon you know some new things. You look at the book again and you see that what you thought the book was the day you finished it and what it is don't quite match up. So, you go at it again. And again, if you must. Until it is as close as possible to the novel you came to understand it was meant to be.

Short stories happen exactly the same way. They just don't take as long.

When Do I Put in the Symbols?

MY FIRST (NEVER PUBLISHED) NOVEL WAS TITLED *Family Matters.* The day I finished it, I went to the drug store, where, browsing the paperback rack for a book to treat myself with, I saw one titled... *Family Matters.*

I freaked out.

Not that it was the greatest title in the world. It wasn't. But it had been the title in my mind the whole time I was writing the book. I liked the little play on words: *family* matters, family *matters*. I didn't know then that you can't copyright a book title—meaning, I could still have used it if I'd wanted to. So I calmed down and started trying to think of a new one.

I decided on *Family Patterns*. It conveyed the idea that families have patterns of thought and behavior. It also occurred to me that it was a tradition in some families to pass a set of "good china" down through generations of daughters, and that the design on a piece of good china is called its pattern. There was a holiday scene in the book, and I figured I could tweak it, underpinning this idea, if I had the daughter bring her mother a new piece of good family china as a gift.

Then I got stuck. What kind of china pattern would the family in my book have? They weren't wealthy or even firmly middle class, so it couldn't be expensive. And the pattern still had to be available for purchase. (This was 1987—so, no miraculous eBay finds.)

I set off for a local department store that carried an extensive collection of china and explained my dilemma to a saleslady. She was intrigued. She showed me numerous patterns; I took notes. Moving from one case to the next, she suddenly stopped. "About that last one," she said. "I should tell you that the mold was broken during World War II. So, while you can still buy the pattern, collectors know the difference between pieces made before and after the war."

Holy cow! I thought.

At its heart, my book was about a young woman—a college student—coming of age during the 1960s and struggling to find a connection with her World War II–generation mother. In a sense, the whole book was about how a mold had been broken—how girls coming up in the 1960s just weren't going to be the women their mothers expected them to be.

It was all I could do not to laugh, imagining students reading my book years later, their English teacher saying, "Why did the author choose that particular china pattern, knowing the mold had been broken during World War II? What did that pattern symbolize?" And my ghost-self whispering, "It was total coincidence. The writer never would have known this if the saleslady hadn't told her. She didn't have a clue."

"It isn't like you're hiding symbols for an Easter egg hunt," short story writer Stuart Dybek said on the topic of symbolism. "It's happening naturally because you're creating images in this believable way and all of this other stuff is just by-products."

Of course, once those symbols find their way in there, you can revise the story to make them stronger. Then again, you might be completely unaware of them. In fact, some writers don't recognize the symbols in their own published stories—and are surprised when readers and critics bring them to their attention.

So, just write. Let the story in process give you the symbols. Then do your best to make them sing.

Working (a Jigsaw)

THE SKY WAS ICY BLUE. THE LINE of trees across the meadow seemed engraved on it, their charcoal trunks dark against the snow.

Inside, the wood stove burned brightly. A whole week in this cozy cabin stretched before me, with nothing to do but write.

I unpacked my computer and a dozen or so books about the Dutch painter Johannes Vermeer, whose imaginary daughter Carelina was the main character in the novel I was writing. I had also brought several postcards of his paintings, pages and pages of research, and a jigsaw puzzle of "The Music Lesson."

In the painting, a woman wearing a vivid red skirt stands at a harpsichord, her back turned to the viewer, a honey-colored cello abandoned at her feet. To her right, between the harpsichord and a framed portrait, a man dressed in black—perhaps Vermeer himself—watches her. The placement of furniture and objects—the cello, a blue upholstered chair with lion's head finials—creates a kind of barrier between the man and the woman, but the mirror above the harpsichord reveals the woman's interest in her companion. This intimate detail, and the glimpse of an easel in the top-right corner of the mirror, turn the world of the painting inside out.

"Remember me," Vermeer seems to be saying. "I made this."

I hadn't worked on a puzzle since I was a child—and I hadn't much liked doing it then. It seemed like an absurd activity for an adult. I'd bought this one because I couldn't quit looking at the beautiful picture on the box; then I'd put it on a shelf in my office and forgotten all about it. Gathering my things for my week of solitude, I noticed the puzzle on the shelf and added it to my bag, thinking maybe I'd work on it when I needed a break.

I was overwhelmed when I opened the cellophane package of puzzle pieces and spilled them out on the table. There were so many of them, and each one so small! Then I noticed a gold piece with scrolling on it and recognized it as part of the harpsichord the woman in the painting plays. I saw another piece of harpsichord, and another. I was surprised at the chord of satisfaction that resonated inside me when these pieces interlocked. I couldn't help searching out another, then another, and another, and another until the harpsichord began to emerge. Oh! And there was a buttery yellow piece with faint orange markings—clearly part of one of the letters on the raised lid of the instrument.

In the next days, I couldn't pass the table without stopping to add more pieces to the puzzle. I studied each piece intently—its color, its shape, its markings—looking for clues to the whole. A dash of orange, a thin green line, a silver curve. An eye? A fret? A finger? But so many of the pieces I picked up seemed almost identical—and at the same time were maddeningly unique. Hours and hours I'd meant to spend writing *Vermeer's Daughter* passed as I stood staring at the picture of his painting, then at some section of the puzzle I was trying to complete.

I thought of an early scene in the novel, when Carelina wakes at dawn and follows her father to the building inside which he is painting "View of Delft." He shows her how he will use a camera obscura to cast the image of the street below onto the huge canvas pinned to the wall

"It is a kind of magic, what you will see inside," he said. "Do not be afraid."

I was never afraid when I was with him. Still, when we entered the room and he closed the door behind us, I trembled to see our town of Delft again, this time floating before me in utter darkness.

The water in the harbor sparkled. Dots of light were strung across a blue herring boat near the Rotterdam Gate and along the rooftops, like little pearls. In the distance, the spire of the Nieuwe Kerk was so bright that it seemed to have been touched by the hand of God.

In time, she becomes her father's apprentice.

Now, I imagined Carelina watching her father prepare the scene on the puzzle box. He places the table, the cello, the mirror, the rug, the harpsichord, the chair just so. He directs the man closer, then farther from the instrument. Using the palm of his hand, he gently turns the woman's face this way and that. At last, every little thing seems to him in harmony with the immutable angles and patterns in the floor, the roof beams, the walls, the windows. So, he steps out of the picture, picks up his brush, and dips it to the palette Carelina has mixed for him.

Color against color: I once read that Vermeer accomplished his magical effect not by looking at the objects he painted, but at the way the colors of an object lay, one against another, on a plane. He built paintings with color. It was a process not so different from putting together a jigsaw puzzle, I thought—until I searched the palette of puzzle pieces for the luminous colors in the painting. There were a few yellow pieces, a few solidly red ones, that could be easily placed. But most were, at best, an undefined mush of color. Three bright dots on one piece suggested upholstery tacks; this told me that it probably made up part of the blue chair. But how? The puzzle piece wasn't blue; it was more like steel gray. And yet, when I placed the piece against another one with similar dots, blue emerged as surely and suddenly as if a chemical reaction had occurred.

Sometimes, I stared back and forth from painting to puzzle, thinking there must be pieces missing. There couldn't possibly be enough blue pieces to make the second chair, for instance. But I believed in magic now. I kept on, quickening when I found more gold dots on a few dark pieces. These were part of a second blue chair, I thought—farther back in the scene, next to the man. I put them together, waiting for the moment they'd morph to blue before my eyes. But this time, it didn't happen. No matter how I looked at it, the second chair in the puzzle was not blue. But I'd seen blue when I first noticed the chair in the painting; I saw blue now when I stepped away. Was this a trick of the eye? Had Vermeer somehow simply *suggested* blue? Was it because I recognized the chair as the same blue Vermeer painted again and again? If I'd never seen that blue—never heard of Vermeer or seen his work before that moment—would I have seen something *other* than blue?

Then I wondered, Was seeing blue that wasn't there comparable to reading between the lines in a story?

Occasionally, I picked up a piece and saw immediately where it should go. Sometimes, I looked at a piece for what seemed like forever, trying to make it fit in every feasible space but ultimately setting it aside because it didn't seem to belong anywhere. Sometimes, when I correctly placed one piece, it became obvious where a number of others would fit around it—which I found thrilling. Sometimes, a piece seemed to fit, but didn't—something I realized only later, which forced me to disassemble the whole section and do it over. It comforted me in my frustration to remember that an X-ray of the real painting showed that Vermeer himself had reworked the position of the man, the girl's head, the lid of the harpsichord, the neck of the pitcher.

I began to feel at least somewhat redeemed for all the writing time I'd wasted when I realized that looking from puzzle to painting again and again was teaching me something about the way Vermeer carried information from his eye to the brush. Just as I had to look at the pieces one at a time to complete the puzzle, he had painted each object in the picture by looking at it spot by spot. This helped me understand why the pieces that made the shadowy gray wall beneath the window were green. Why some of the black tile pieces were green and others were charcoal. Why the white tiles weren't white at all, but a swirl of light and dark gray.

And the light! If I was confounded by how Vermeer made these vivid objects out of what seemed like no real color at all, how could I ever hope to understand how he painted the golden light seeping in through the window? If I held two puzzle pieces in my hand—one from the most luminous section of the wall and another from the section near the mirror where the light has begun to fade—I could see they were completely different shades of yellow. Yet, looking at the place in the painting where the two sections meet, and at each of the sections itself, I couldn't see where the light began to change.

I looked harder, but the essence of the light simply would not reveal itself. I had an odd thought then: *What if it never revealed itself to Vermeer, either?* What if it had felt like failure to him to accept that seeing the way light lay against not-light was as close as he would ever come to defining it? That luminosity was some trick of the Earth itself, from which both the painter and the paints were made?

Was this something I needed to know to bring Vermeer alive in my book?

If so, did that mean I'd been working, after all?

As I concentrated on each puzzle piece, trying to find its right place, insights, images, and ideas for the novel floated up, not unlike pieces of a puzzle. A girl following her father in the early morning, a girl as real and as vivid as my own two daughters in a favorite photo of them sitting on my desk. The tall, peaked buildings of 16th-century Delft, a quiet room with an easel, a clock tower, a wind sled on a frozen canal.

I looked up, beyond the words and the puzzle, to the winter scene outside my window, and the whole world fractured. The window frame dissolved to a kind of bargello in shades of brown. The braided cord of the Venetian blind was no more than a simple red line, hatched with bright, whitened-red, and outlined in a thread of pure white. The push pin holding the cord in place was made of a dot of white, a half-moon of lemon-yellow, and a slice of duller yellow mixed with black. Outside, the snow falling was a swirling tapestry of silver, white, and gray.

As each piece of the puzzle fell into its right place, revealing, suddenly, the corner where the line of roof timbers met the window casing, or the man's face, or the crisscross pattern on the back of the woman's gown, I felt some small measure of what I was certain Vermeer had felt the moment when, after a long patience, the small slice of the world he was looking at yielded to his brush. It was the way I felt myself as pieces of a novel came together, eventually revealing the whole.

Finished on the last day of my solitude, my completed puzzle seemed a work of art in its own right. The colors were luminous, the pattern of pieces effected a kind of cracquelature on the surface, and, at that moment, I was as pleased as the Queen herself must be to own something so beautiful. The puzzle became a piece of my life. An object. A lesson.

The many pieces of a story gather themselves into being, each piece complete in its own way, utterly, maddeningly, gloriously itself. Work is whatever helps brings those pieces to the surface of your mind and turn them into words.

Mind the Gap

I NEVER REALLY KNEW MY ENGLISH GRANDPARENTS, but they always sent us Christmas gifts when I was a child. The best were the creamy Macintosh toffees in red-wrapped rolls and books with stories about rosy-cheeked English children who went on holiday instead of vacation, wore jumpers instead of sweaters, played in gardens instead of yards, and donned macs and wellies to go out in the rain.

I particularly loved listening to my mom's stories about England during the war—friends and family and neighbors drinking tea and knitting in the bomb shelters during the Blitz. One time, a bomb went straight through her grandparents' house, from attic to basement; incredibly, it did not detonate. I imagined my mom emerging among the bomb craters after the "all-clear" to catch the double-decker bus that passed over Westminster Bridge and Big Ben every morning to her job at a dress shop.

I wanted to go to England more than anything, but I didn't

get there until I was in my thirties. I remember waking on the airplane near the end of the long flight to the pilot's voice saying, "If you look out the window, you can see England beneath you." I was almost afraid to look. What if it turned out to be just like everywhere else? But it wasn't! Peering down, I saw a beautiful green patchwork of fields, winding roads, here and there villages with red brick houses. I felt like I'd come home.

Everything delighted me. The bustle of London—double-decker buses careening around corners, fleets of black taxis like big birds flying along the streets. The changing of the guard at Buckingham Palace, the Tower of London with the chopping block on which two of King Henry the VIII's six wives were beheaded. Cozy tea rooms, hot buttered scones.

I laughed the first time I saw a "Mind the Gap" sign in a London Tube station. It was meant as a warning to watch out for the gap between the platform and the train. But the phrase made its way into the mix of stuff inside my head, emerging at some point as the perfect metaphor for revision. That is, as a writer, you must mind the gap between the story you have in your head and heart and the one you've managed to transfer to the page in words.

This gap is not evidence of failure. It's fundamental to the process of translating ideas to words. Revision is about identifying the problems that create that gap, and then developing a strategy to solve them one-by-one—narrowing it so the reader won't fall through the story into confusion. This is what gives a story its polish and makes it feel seamless and real. Accepting criticism from readers who ask questions and make observations is essential. Useful criticism can help you understand the nature of the gap, and should always be received as a gift.

The idea of closing this gap *after* writing your story is completely opposite of what I learned in school. Our teachers told us to make an outline of what we wanted to say and then fill it in. Revision simply meant going back in to correct grammar, punctuation, and spelling errors. Then, we were told to recopy the story neatly and turn it in. Asking for help in this process was cheating. So was writing first and *then* outlining—something I did regularly, and guiltily.

The idea that writing before outlining was cheating was so ingrained in me in school that it thwarted my courage to write for years—and undermined my ability to write with confidence once I finally started. This was complicated by the implication that I was supposed to know what I was going to write *before* I wrote it and by the idea that getting any kind of feedback was cheating. I realize now that my lack of confidence went all the way back to the rejection of *Slave Girl,* that earnest but misconceived novel of my childhood. *You're too stupid to be a writer*, I told myself then—and quit for twenty years. But, eventually, a time came when not writing no longer felt like an option.

So I gathered up my courage and jumped right into writing a novel. I loved reading novels; I was addicted to them. I'd wanted to write novels for as long as I could remember. To me, a story is a snack, while a novel is a full buffet of life. Still operating under the illusion that writing was all about talent, completely unaware that writing fiction was a craft to be learned, it never occurred to me that starting with the shorter form might be a good idea.

Hindsight tells me there are benefits to starting with short stories—the main one being that you fail more quickly. Short stories don't take as long to write as novels, and they can teach you a lot about the basic elements of fiction that will serve you well when you feel ready to take on what one friend of mine calls "The Long Thing." A good workshop, writing group, or reader can help you identify what's working in your story and what's not, and you can revise it and move on to the next one. If you learn from your mistakes, your writing will improve with each new attempt.

Novels are a whole different thing. They take a long time to write and a long time to revise. You can ask your readers to critique your novel as you go, but novels often change in process, making early critiques useless—even confusing. But asking them to read a finished draft is asking them for a *lot* of their time. Plus, it's considerably more difficult to critique a novel than a story because you must be able to hold the whole thing in your head, while at the same time seeing each part distinctly and how it relates to the others. No small task.

But the gap is the gap, no matter the form. You must learn strategies to make it as narrow as it can be—and be grateful for those few gifted readers who can help along the way. If you are fortunate enough to sell your book and feel discouraged when your editor asks for even more revisions, remember this: Nine times out of ten, good editors are right.

The Revision Toolkit

"EVERY STORY TEACHES ME HOW TO WRITE it," Eudora Welty said. "Unfortunately, it doesn't teach me how to write the next one."

Nor does revising one story teach you to revise the one that follows it. This is why every writer needs a revision toolkit, and the wherewithal to create new tools when necessary to suit the unique problems of a story.

The first tool in any revision toolkit (and the easiest one to use) is putting the manuscript away for a while—at least a month, maybe more. Later, when you pull it back out and reread it, you'll see all kinds of things that demand to be fixed. Rereading and marking up the manuscript is rarely enough, though. The task is so tedious that eventually you start skimming and lose the level of concentration you need to see what's there. So, you need other tools at your disposal.

My own best revision tool was born of desperation—when nothing I knew or thought I knew could help me see what I needed to see to fix a novel I'd been working on for years. All I could think to do was to write down the first sentence of the first chapter. Then, on the next line, I wrote, "page one." I looked at this a while, then jotted down a shorthand version of what happened on that page. After that I wrote, "page two" and did the same. After I'd described what happened on each page, I wrote the last sentence of the chapter. Then I skipped a line and did the same with chapter 2, chapter 3, chapter 4—all the way through the manuscript.

It took forever. It made me feel crazy. But I kept going because it was better than sitting and staring, confused and downhearted. Then a strange thing began to happen: The more I wrote down the obvious, the more new ideas and useful observations popped up. Like, character X seems to have disappeared. Is that a problem? Or, this flashback is going on for pages. Or, yoo-hoo, didn't you use the same description a couple of chapters ago?

I jotted these things down and kept going. Days later, when I wrote the last sentence of the last chapter, I was surprised to find that all these jottings comprised a list of issues to consider in deciding what needed to be revised. How cool is that? I thought.

But before proceeding, I free-wrote about the book—what I had noticed, whatever came to mind. This yielded even more insights, questions, and observations, and even a few solutions.

I used all this information to make a very specific list of what I wanted to look at closely. Then, I chose one issue on the list, got out my highlighters, and highlighted each line in the book where it appeared. I did this with every issue on the list, giving each one its own color. When I ran out of highlighter colors, I used assorted colors of ink, circles, X's, asterisks—whatever I could think of. As I did this, yet more useful observations surfaced.

When I finished all the highlighting and marking, I laid the pages out like a carpet runner. I was astonished to see that they made a map of the novel. I could see how the various elements I'd tracked moved through it—where they were and where they weren't. I could see what was in balance and where I needed to create balance. I could see where last lines did not echo first lines, where scenes were needed to break up narrative. I could see where promises made and questions raised in the beginning were left dangling by the end, like errant strands of a braid. The colorful, marked-up manuscript was beautiful, its own little work of art.

Now I do this with all my novels. In an early draft of *Everything You Want*, a novel about a family that goes berserk after winning fifty million in the lottery, one issue I highlighted was where the money came into play (in green, of course). When I finished, I noticed that there were solid chunks of green early on, but that by chapter eight, they had dwindled to just a few lines. I'd gotten so interested in the characters and their various problems that I'd forgotten about the money. So, one of my revision tasks was to go back and find ways to pull the issue of money all the way through to the end of the book.

I refined this exercise over the years, going from handwriting to typing—and, finally, to spreadsheets, a format I've found beneficial in various ways. Using a spreadsheet, I can track characters in columns and easily experiment with chapter placement. Recently, having puzzled a long time over where three different chapters fit into the book you're reading now, I gave each one a color and put them in all the places I thought they might work. The very instant I placed the third piece in the third spot—boom! I knew exactly where each one was meant to be.

I have no idea what's happening in my head at these moments, but I count on them to teach me what I need to know. The whole process is about trusting that if you muster up the mind-numbing discipline to work through your story page-by-page, some gear in your brain will eventually shift, taking you to a place where discipline and instinct merge. The rush of questions and observations that come with this shift reveal the gap between your idea and the words you've used to express it and offer steppingstones to help you cross it.

It's not magic. Doing this exercise is a long, crazy-making slog. And working your way through the list of revision tasks doesn't ensure you will have solved all of your novel's problems. In fact, it's likely that solving some problems will reveal or create new ones. It's not unusual to have to do this exercise numerous times, drafting and redrafting until that moment when you've made the gap between the story in your head and the one on the page as narrow as it can be. Nonetheless, it remains the best antidote to sitting and staring I know.

Sometimes, especially with later drafts, I use big index cards in a shortened version of this exercise, allotting one card for each chapter. On each card, I summarize the plot of the chapter, and write the answers to the following questions (and any others that come to mind):

- Who's present?
- How many scenes are in the chapter?
- What's the balance of scene and narrative?
- How much time does the chapter cover in the now of the novel?
- How many levels of time do flashbacks represent?
- What's introduced?
- What's left hanging?
- What's resolved?
- What's at stake in the chapter?
- Where are the moments of tension?
- Where does the chapter torque and surprise?

As in the more extensive "outline," I jot down observations that float up as I go.

You can also use index cards to help you decide on the sequence of scenes, using one card for each scene. In this case, you write a summary of the scene and answer any questions from the preceding list. As you go, you can also note observations about character, time, and place. Then play with the cards. Organize them in a variety of ways to help you discover the best order for them to appear in the novel—or to decide whether they need to appear at all.

If you're using multiple points of view in your novel, give each point of view character a different colored index card, then arrange all the cards in chronological order to see the sequence of points of view and consider whether they are balanced appropriately throughout the book.

Making a timeline helps you see what's happening when and can help clarify the backstory. It can also reveal patterns, logistical problems, or places where you might add new material. Your timeline can cover just the timeframe of the novel or the time from when significant events in the backstory occur through to the resolution. You can list in chronological order the hours, days, months, or years you want to consider, and then add the important events of the story.

A timeline is especially useful if your backstory runs deep. Give each character a column that begins at the age at which he or she enters the story. From there, number down to the year the novel ends to see the characters' comparative ages at crucial moments of the story. This is helpful in ensuring that references to your characters in the now of the story make sense. It may also generate ideas that merge the characters' pasts in new and important ways.

Making an actual calendar of your novel's timeframe and putting scenes on it can bring insights about pace. The blank days between scenes help you see where transitions and narrative passages are needed.

Other revision tools include charts and maps. Charts can show each character's motives, emotions, what they know, and their whereabouts when on and offstage in the novel, which can be useful in plotting. A map of your novel's setting—whether it's a town, a neighborhood, a farm with outbuildings, a house, or even a single room—can help you see the proximity of people, places, and events, and to move characters through the physical world of the story.

When researching to solve problems of authenticity, stay open to serendipity. Sometimes, looking for what you need to know reveals something you'd never have thought to look for—and might even uncover a solution to the problem you set out to solve or reveal a problem you didn't know was there.

Read your work aloud. Better yet, have someone read it to you. You'll hear what's wrong—especially those wrong notes in voice and tone.

I know. It's mind-boggling to consider all the things that might be wrong with a story. It's overwhelming to think about how to start identifying these problems—let alone how to solve them. But unless you commit to this process, it's virtually impossible to write a story that will not only make readers keep turning the pages, but illuminate the world we share.

"And though the rewriting—and the rereading—sound like effort, they are actually the most pleasurable parts of writing," Susan Sontag wrote. "Sometimes the only pleasurable parts."

Really? You may be thinking. Was she serious?

She was.

I agree with her. In fact, revision can be *delicious*:

The pleasure in choosing just the right color to represent each problem.

The colorful, marked-up outline laid out, talking to me.

Excitement about beginning again, the belief that I can make the story better.

The headiness of cutting when, finally, I know what needs to be cut, and hearing the remaining words sing.

And the opposite: conjuring a scene for the sole purpose of slowing down the pace that, in the process of being written, yields the resolution of a crucial issue and makes me wonder how in the world I had failed to realize that I needed this scene from the get-go.

A transition falling into place like a little bridge.

And, best of all, the thrilling *Whoa!* when, suddenly, I hold the whole novel in my head—a gargantuan, incandescent web, quivering with life. I know where everything is; I know what it all means.

Revising is hard. It's tedious and frustrating work. But for me, it makes the book seem possible. Writing, I feel like a blind person tapping my way through a foreign world. I feel untalented, insecure, even unworthy. Who am I even to *attempt* a novel, when so many extraordinary novels by extraordinary writers already exist? The black hole I must fill with story sometimes makes me feel hopeless. But revising, I feel like a repair person with a full toolkit at hand. I have a list of things to do and confidence that I have the discipline, stubbornness, and passion to work through them—no matter how long it takes. And that this will bring the novel closer to how it feels inside me.

How do I know, finally, when a book is finished?

I never know for sure.

But when I've done every single thing I know to do, I send it out into the world with a prayer that the cosmos will bless its journey.

The Writing Life

New York, New York

FINALLY, I WAS A BONA FIDE WRITER in New York! I arrived at Harper & Row on East 54th Street in New York City on a January morning in 1982, and was escorted to the office of my editor, where stacks of manuscripts towered perilously on every surface. C was in her late forties. She wore a paisley dress, high boots, and a shawl. I instantly adored her—and her husband, M., who ambled in when C. called to him. He was older than she, wearing a rumpled suit and a flowered bow tie.

M. loved my novel, *Night Watch*, which, he described as "spare, economical, elegant." He said C. had given him the manuscript to read and, twenty or so pages in, he had hollered at her from another room, "Who is this Barbara Shoup person, anyway? Where did she come from?"

I was thrilled. And embarrassed.

He grinned at me. "Smile," he said. "It's OK. It's a wonderful book."

C and I lunched at the St. Regis. Then we went back to her office and worked on the manuscript for the rest of the afternoon. "Just a few things to tighten up," she said. That evening, we went to the ballet together. Afterward, we ended up in a coffee shop eating grilled cheese sandwiches and talking about our lives. The next day, it was back to the St. Regis for me—this time for lunch with my agent, R., to sign the contract.

Afterwards, walking up 5th Avenue on the way back to my hotel, I marveled at the ease with which my book had made its way to this center of the universe of words. R. had been among the first batch of agents to whom I'd sent my first novel. She'd responded quickly with a letter asking to represent me. That first book never sold, but when I completed *Night Watch*, it was picked up by Harper & Row within a month.

I was on my way.

When the book came out the following fall, the reviews—including a starred review in *Publishers Weekly*—were excellent. But sales were modest, at best. I soon learned that the shelf life for novels with modest sales is about three months. In some cases, any books left over after that period are simply shredded. Others, like mine, were "remaindered"—sold to bookstores for their bargain book tables, each one the death of an author's dream made visible.

"What should I do to promote my writing career?" I asked C. afterward, thinking there was something I should have done for *Night Watch* that I hadn't known to do.

"Writers don't have careers," C. said. "They write."

So, I wrote.

Twelve years passed before the publication of my next novel.

It was a bad time. I worked constantly. When I wasn't working, I was distracted—often deeply depressed. I dreaded the question, "When is your next novel coming out?" But it was even worse when people *quit* asking, apparently having concluded it was never going to happen.

I kept going. If I stopped, who would I be?

For most of that period, I worked on *Stranded in Harmony*. C. read draft after draft of that book, making copious notes on each one. She continued to believe in the book—to believe in me. But five years passed. Even I knew this could not go on forever. Finally, C. had no choice but to let the book go. When she did, she wrote to my new agent, A.:

Barbara is a writer, a very, very good one, and I know a lot about her: I know that she won't be defeated by this setback, and I know that in her long future there are going to be many good books. I hope I'll get to publish them. But there are moments in a novelist's life where it's the wrong time for a certain story, or books that simply refuse to be born... This may be the case here, or it may be that there is some way to fix this story that Barbara and I together couldn't find.

I was heartbroken, but I knew that C. had been right to release it.

Several more years passed. My agent sent the book out to more than twenty editors, only to have it returned—often with complimentary rejections. Here was the most maddening among them:

I loved this one. Let me say that again. I loved this one! It was one of those special novels that I hoped against hope I would be able to buy. However, I did not get the same reaction in readings from the powers that be, and so, I am forced to send this lovely gem back to you.

About six years into this twelve-year period, I visited New York—this time just for fun. During my visit, I saw a Broadway musical called *Sunday in the Park with George*, about the post-Impressionist painter Georges Seurat. I'm not usually a fan of musical theater...and I don't often cry. But as this play unfolded, I found myself captivated. When the curtain fell, I was in tears.

"Order. Design. Tension. Composition. Balance. Light. Harmony." Seurat repeats these words like a mantra throughout the play. His obsession with them makes him an observer rather than a participant in life. It also drives him to create the painting that will be recognized as a masterpiece after his death: "A Sunday Afternoon on the Island of La Grande Jatte." But in the process, Seurat endures poverty, ridicule, and despair. He loses the woman he loves—and who loves him. He tries and fails, tries and fails to balance life and art.

This same pattern lives on in Seurat's fictional great-grandson, George. The play's second act finds the contemporary George at the crowded opening of an exhibit of his work. He should be happy—critics marvel at his art, reviewers crowd in for quotes. But success and its increasing expectations, the phoniness of the art world, paralyze him. Amidst the clamor all around him, his voice growing stronger as he speaks, he recites what his grandmother said about Seurat:

"Order. Design. Tension. Composition. Balance. Light. Harmony.

"White. A blank canvas. His favorite. So many possibilities."

I can't say exactly what it was about the play that hit me so hard. Maybe it was watching the grief and confusion I felt in my own struggle to balance my art and my life—and my desire for recognition—play out on the stage. Maybe it was fear. All those years I had clung to the belief that every good book would eventually find its place in the world, but was I was beginning to see that I might be wrong about that.

I *was* wrong about it. Wonderful books go unpublished. Gifted writers receive little or no recognition for their work.

Even as this began to be painfully clear to me, I kept on. I wrote another (failed) novel. I started yet another that stopped in its tracks. Then, suddenly, an idea I'd been noodling around with for a while offered me a thread to follow. I wrote like crazy. I finished that novel, called *Wish You Were Here*, in less than a year.

There was just one problem: The main character of that book was a teenager. "People don't want to read about teenagers," my agent, A., said. But another agent, M., was certain she could sell it—and did, almost immediately. The publisher was a new Disney imprint called Hyperion; they wanted to publish the book as a young adult novel.

I worried about being pigeonholed as a YA author, but I was hungry for a second publication. So, I said yes—and the decision was a good one. *Wish You Were Here* got way more attention as a YA novel than it would have as a novel for adults. It got great reviews. It was named a 1994 Best Book for Young Adults by the American Library Association, a Blue Ribbon Book by the Center for Children's Books, and a Best Young Adult Book by the Voice of Youth Advocates. It was even optioned for television.

When Hyperion asked for another novel, it occurred to me that there might be hope for *Stranded in Harmony* yet—and created a synopsis with the teenage boy, Lucas, as the main character. My editor liked it, so I went back to work on the book. Hyperion accepted the manuscript and listed the book for the following fall.

Then, Hyperion cleaned house, firing most of the staff—including my editor.

Fortunately, the new editor assigned to *Stranded in Harmony* liked it well enough to hang on to it, but she took it off the fall list. She thought it needed considerably more work—and sent me eight single-spaced pages of notes explaining why.

I swore upon receiving the critique. A *lot*. I was also confused. How was I supposed to know what to think about my book when two equally qualified editors felt so differently about it? I considered withdrawing the book, but that would be iffy. The thought of another long process of rejection was just too horrible to contemplate. So, I tackled the changes she asked for. And, back in process, my understanding of the book shifted. Suddenly, I saw how to solve a problem that I realized had been there all along. Ultimately, *Stranded in Harmony* was named an ALA Best Book for Young Adults, appeared on the International Reading Association Choice List and The Children's Choice List, and was a finalist for the Great Lakes Book Award for Young Adult Fiction.

Between 1997 and 2005, I published two more novels: *Faithful Women* and *Vermeer's Daughter*. I also co-authored *Novel Ideas* and *Story Matters*, about the creative process. In 2006, I won the PEN Phyllis Reynolds Naylor Working Writer Fellowship for *Everything You Want*, a young adult novel published in 2008. *An*

American Tune followed in 2012 and *Looking for Jack Kerouac* in 2014. As I type this, several other novels are out there looking for homes; others are in process.

All this looks great on paper. But when I add up the income I've earned from my writing for over four decades, it averages out to about $2,600 a year. Some days, I look at my books lined up on the shelf and feel good about what I've accomplished. Other days I feel like a complete and total loser. On those days, I tell myself what I tell aspiring writers: There's no ladder to climb in the arts. There's very little logic in why some writers become rich and famous and other, often better, writers remain unsung or even destitute. There is no reliable measure of success by any standard other than your own. And there are factors at work in who does and does not succeed that may be unknown to you.

Years ago, I met a writer whose first collection of short stories had been published to great acclaim. At that time, he was desperately struggling to finish his first novel. A few years later, he appeared on a prestigious list of Best Young American Novelists. The next time we met, I congratulated him and said I looked forward to reading the book. Mortified, he replied, "Oh, God. I still haven't finished it." In fact, his novel wasn't published for another five years. Digging a little, I learned he was a protégé of an icon of contemporary American fiction. This probably had something to do with how he got on that list of Best Young American Novelists. The discovery made me feel more relieved than angry. There was a pretty good chance that at least *some* of my failure to achieve recognition as a novelist had little or nothing to do with the books themselves.

There are ways to be savvy as a writer, ways to increase the likelihood that your work will be recognized. But promoting myself is not my strong suit. It doesn't help that the three cardinal rules of my upbringing were 1) never brag, 2) never admit you need anything, and 3) *for God's sake*, never ask for money.

Then there's the fact that writing takes me out of the real world, which is why I love and need it. Once a novel is finished, I'm on to the next one—and that world is so much more compelling than the world of marketing, the exact opposite of the creative process that keeps me in balance and makes me feel whole.

But these days, the meager marketing budgets for all but a few works of fiction require writers to be marketers, regardless of their skills in this area. Months before the publication of a book, writers spend hours and hours lobbying for readings, reviews, interviews, book signings, guest blog posts. They post the book jacket on social media, tweet every positive comment that comes their way. Then, when the novel finally arrives in the world, they spend the next year being a capital-A author, doing all the interviews and book signings and other events they set up beforehand, and feeling guilty about all the stuff they *should* have set up but didn't get around to—no doubt because they were in such a state of anxiety and exhaustion from publishing a book they feared would be ignored.

And of course, all during this time, they've had very little time to write.

Some very good writers have a knack for marketing—even enjoy it. There are certainly book events I enjoy myself: the book launch, when friends and family gather to celebrate the birth of the new book; attending book club meetings and engaging in lively discussions with members who read the book; visiting high schools and universities to talk with students who studied the book in class.

But a lot of book events leave me feeling catatonic. The worst was arriving for a book signing at a local bookstore only to discover they'd forgotten to put the event on their schedule. There was no table available to use, and the few copies of the book that the store had on hand were propped up in a Local Author display in the window. So, they set me in a rolling office chair by the store entrance, plucked a copy of the novel from the display, and handed it to me—thinking, I guess, that I could accost people entering the store and make a sales pitch. Instead, customers assumed I was part of the staff. "Where are the Garfield books?" one asked. "Could you tell me where I can find *Thinner Thighs in 30 Days*?" asked another. I sold one book, to a friend's mother—and went home and took to my bed.

Being a writer is not for the faint of heart. This truth is difficult to convey to aspiring writers, so many of whom believe—as I once did—that writing will bring them fame and fortune. It's difficult to find a balance between being honest with these hopeful writers about the realities of writing and selling fiction and freaking them out so badly they'll never even try. So, I follow that age-old maxim of writing: show, don't tell. That is, I show them a photo of myself standing next to a pile of all the failed drafts of *Stranded in Harmony*, the novel that took me the longest to write. The pile reaches my shoulder.

I especially get a kick out of showing this photo to high school students during author visits. Invariably, some kid will ask, "Why didn't you just quit?"

"Excellent question," I say. "I didn't quit because those characters were all alive in my head, and they'd still be there, ghosts, making me feel awful if I had abandoned them." Then I talk about what it's like to live in the real world *and* the worlds inside my head, how each world feeds the other, how writing feels like cheating death sometimes—living lives other than my own.

How, when I'm in a world of my own making, I don't care about the book business at all.

The Voices in My Head

DRIVING ONE DAY, NPR ON THE RADIO, I heard a voice say, "Nobody knows what it's like to be a writer but another writer." *Damn right*, I thought. Then laughed when I realized the voice had been mine—a sound bite promoting an arts program I'd been interviewed on a few months before.

Still, it's true. "Regular" people just don't understand.

This is why it's so important to have a community of writers—people who know how it feels to do what you do and why it matters. Voices you can count on to say, "I know." "I get it." "Carry on." "*Yes*."

A chorus of those voices rises in my head when I need them most, to drown out the voices of doubt and discouragement.

"This anonymous person is a *writer*," the editor of the *Saturday Evening Post* said of a short piece I'd slipped in among submissions from student writers in a community class I'd organized. I didn't out myself, but he knew—and I felt, for the first time, hopeful.

"You need an agent," said the professor to whom I'd submitted my first novel as an independent study student. "It's good." It was the first time I'd shown the book to anyone but family or friends.

"You're a novelist," said the instructor in the graduate short story workshop I joined the next semester. "It's fine to bring in chapters instead of stories."

I took classes at the Indiana Writers Center, where instructors and classmates encouraged me. I attended writers' conferences, where I met like-minded writers and formed friendships that sustain me to this day.

Not long after *Night Watch* came out, I received a letter from a writer who'd won the National Book Award several years before. She wanted me to know how much she loved the book. This kindness astonished me. I wrote to thank her, she wrote back, and we began a correspondence about our work that was punctuated by occasional long phone conversations, back when long-distance phone calls cost a fortune.

Since those early days, my community of writers has grown. Some of its members live nearby, while others are in far-flung places. And I meet new writers all the time—some of whom merely pass through my life while others become essential to it. I especially love when my students become fellow writers.

I never had a writing group until recently, when three other women and I decided to give it a try. Since then, all of us have written more than we would have on our own and have benefited immeasurably from the thoughtful critiques of our work. The benefit we *hadn't* counted on—although it has turned out to be the most important of all—is the *yes*, so loud, so sure that it echoes through the days between our meetings.

Yes, you should be writing.

Yes, it's good. Keep going.

Yes, I feel exactly the same way.

Near the end of 2018, I spent three weeks at Ragdale, an artists' retreat where I am always happy. This time, I stayed in the main residence—an Arts and Crafts–style house that had once been the summer estate of a wealthy Chicago family. It's my dream of what a house should be: beautifully appointed, cozy and spacious at the same time, full of color and light. I loved my room, called the Blue Room, with its sprigged blue and white wallpaper and comfy reading chair, my desk overlooking the prairie. I loved coming down to the sunny blue and yellow kitchen—usually in my pajamas, no matter what time of day. I loved stopping in the sunroom before I headed back upstairs, with its Giverny-green tables and chairs, its tall, leggy geraniums blooming all along the windows.

I was totally frazzled when I arrived at Ragdale—overwhelmed with obligations. I felt discouraged about whether I would ever sell a novel again. *You're too old*, said that nasty little voice in my head. *With an abysmal sales record to boot*. But after a few days, writing all day and sometimes into the night, I began to breathe. *So what if I never sell anything again?* I thought. *Writing my novel—living in it—is enough.*

One of the things I love most about Ragdale is the energetic silence—the calm intensity generated by the little community of other artists at work all around me. But I also love the evening meal at the Barn House, where all of us gather around the long table, talking and laughing. During this residency, there was an especially congenial group, all women—eight writers, a dancer/choreographer, a video artist, and a composer. Often, we talked long into the evening. We took walks on the snowy prairie and to Lake Michigan. We shared our work.

It was near Christmas, so we all attended the holiday party together. A Tarot reader had been brought in, and a bunch of us thought, *Why not?* I wish I could remember what cards I drew, how the reader laid them out before me, and what she said about them. But all I remember was her conclusion: It's time to let something go.

I assumed she meant my job at the Indiana Writers Center, where I'd served as the executive director for the past ten years. At Ragdale, I had remembered what it was like to be a writer—to write with no other obligation than the story unfolding in my head. To write without worrying about marketing, fundraising, programs, and all the other large and small matters that ate up my hours and cluttered my mind in my capacity of executive director. If I gave up that position, time would open up like the prairie beyond the Blue Room window.

But later, as we all discussed our Tarot readings in the garden room, I wasn't so sure. The frustration of marketing our work—whether finding an agent or promoting a published book—had been a regular topic among the writers. Everyone hated it. But *they* were doing it…while I was mired in the conviction that trying to find an agent for my work, or even a small publisher, was futile at this point in my career. Suddenly, I thought, *What if the negative voices in my head are what I need to let go of?*

"Why can't you be satisfied with what you have?"

"You're not that good."

"Anyway, it's too late."

"Yes!" my fellow writers said when I shared this insight. "Let those voices go!"

Once, years ago, I made a sixty-minute tape consisting of the Doobie Brothers song "One by One" on repeat for the single line, "You'll always have the chance to give up, so why do it now?" I played the tape running, driving, working out, doing errands, soaking in the bathtub—whenever I felt really discouraged.

I still love that song, but I don't need it like I used to.

Now I listen to the voices saying *yes*.

(Maybe) Don't Quit Your Day Job

IT'S VIRTUALLY IMPOSSIBLE TO MAKE A LIVING *only* writing fiction. That's why most fiction writers I know have a day job—a job they do to earn a living

"You'll need a day job," or "Don't quit your day job," aspiring fiction writers are often warned by the sensible people in their lives—parents, teachers."

"I sure hope he doesn't quit his day job," some say, with a little snicker, talking of a fiction writer who—in their opinion—just isn't any good.

Fiction writers with day jobs might be teachers, editors, publishers, librarians, even freelance nonfiction writers. Or, they might work in unrelated fields: medicine, food service, law, construction, engineering, retail, human resources, science. Writers who patch together a living often like to list the variety of unconventional part-time jobs they've taken to support their writing habit in their bios when they publish their work. House painter, yoga instructor, nanny, waiter, fitness trainer, dog walker, bartender, office cleaner. You name it. Maybe they include the list as a testament to the sacrifices they've made to write, maybe with a sense of irony

Most writers dream of attaining the financial rewards, critical success, and name recognition that would let them write full-time. But what if your day job brings balance to the inevitable frustrations and disappointments of writing? What if it brings moments of pure happiness that living in the world of a story could never bring? What if your day job teaches you about life in a way nothing else could, enriching and complicating your understanding of...well, everything? What if it's the source of some of your best material?

Teaching has given me all of the above for more than forty years. First, I worked in a funky alternative program at a suburban high school that opened my mind to what learning really was and gave me the courage to begin to write. Then I spent twenty years teaching in an urban high school's magnet program for the humanities and performing arts, a job that sustained me when it seemed I'd never publish another book. I've worked as an adjunct instructor at several universities. Now I teach at the Indiana Writers Center, where I began my own writing journey in 1979. The funny thing is, I hadn't been looking for a single one of those jobs—and I didn't even want some of them. But there they were, as if sent by the cosmos to teach me what I didn't know I needed to learn to be a writer.

There have been times I've thought I should give up teaching. *It takes so much time to do it right*, I'd tell myself.

It's emotionally exhausting.

You only do it because it's the one thing you know you do well.

If you were a real writer, you'd quit and find out whether committing to writing full time would improve your writing and finally bring material success.

In fact, more than once, nearing the end of a school year, I told the director of the magnet program I wasn't coming back in the fall. And each time, I showed up in his office after my summer travels and sheepishly asked if it was too late to change my mind.

He'd smile. "I never took you off the roster," he'd say.

The last time I quit and changed my mind, I wrote this in my journal:

> *Trips are so funny. They fade so fast and you're left with a series of images that float up at odd times. I think of the Monet garden, the water lily paintings at the Musée Marmottan Monet in Paris and how I saw them move—understanding, suddenly, his obsession. I think of "View of Delft" and the Van Eyck altarpiece at Ghent. Fields of sunflowers, their heads turned toward the sun. When I got home I had the sudden realization that I needed to teach. It seemed important to me to teach—otherwise, where do all of the lovely images go? The world is such an amazing place and so few people see it. Sometimes I think if someone had only shown me how to see when I was so young and confused and different, it might have made some things bearable. I don't regret having learned what I know so painfully, but I do have some deep need to give it away.*
>
> *For the last year I've had it in my mind that if I wanted to*

be a real writer, I couldn't be the person I was. I had to grow up, stop hanging out with teenagers, get deep. It was time to get serious about writing, do nothing but write. But I love teaching. So much of me is rooted in my impulse to teach, the teaching itself and the relationships that come from it that teaching and writing feel all of a piece to me.

Near the end of my twenty years working in the magnet program, I took my band of teenage writers to Crown Hill Cemetery, a rambling, hilly old graveyard near the center of town. I did this every autumn because writing is about living and dying, and I believed it was useful for us to wander among the graves of those whose lives were over, to feel grateful that we were still here on Earth, living the story of our lives.

This particular year, we made the trip on one of those last almost-warm days. The blue sky was cloudless; the only leaves left on the trees were yellow. I spread a red-checked tablecloth on the grave of James Whitcomb Riley—a famous local poet—slotted a tape of opera arias into the little boom box I'd brought, and we ate lunch. We reveled in the irony of a writing class gathered on the grave of a terrible poet. We talked about things we knew and wished we knew. From where we sat, the city skyline in the distance looked like Oz.

After lunch, I sent the students off with their notebooks to write and reflect—all but one girl, A., whose mother had died of leukemia several years earlier and was buried nearby. I'd brought flowers, and together we took them to A.'s mother's grave. We sat on the warm grass, and A. told me about her mom—what she was like, how much she had loved her and feared losing her. How empty she felt when her mother was finally gone. How, even now, she often couldn't sleep at night. "The worst thing is," she said, "I wonder what my life would have been like if my mother hadn't died, and I can't even imagine it."

I looked away from the pain in her face, searching for something to say, and saw two deer standing among the gravestones in the distance. I touched her shoulder. "Look," I whispered.

As she turned, the deer loped toward us, stopping maybe twenty feet from where we sat. They looked at us for what seemed like forever, then flicked their tails and bounded away on their impossibly delicate legs.

A. looked as if she'd seen a ghost. "Maybe it's stupid," she said. "But do you think that meant something? A kind of sign?"

"Yes," I said. "*Yes.*"

And on that ordinary day, in that unlikely place, I was flooded with light. Again, teaching, I had remembered: It matters to believe in something. To be open to—to be deserving of—the unexpected moment when the world shows its vast, kind spirit.

When I'm feeling low, questioning the decision I made so long ago to keep working in the real world, I remember this moment with A. and the deer at her mother's gravestone. I *can't* know—what would have happened if I'd decided to write full-time. I might be rich and famous, or at least better known. I might be exactly where I am now as a writer—but worse off for having given up that great source of learning about life.

In life there are no revisions. I can't go back and find out.

What a writer's day job teaches her, how it feeds (or impedes) her writing, whether she should or shouldn't work, are just a few more of life's unanswerable questions. I'm just saying, don't give up your day job too fast—especially if it's work you love. Writing full-time is by no means the definition of a serious writer. It's way simpler than that.

Day job or no day job, serious writers choose writing whenever they can.

Three Ways to Look at Being Famous

1.

IN 2015, HARPERCOLLINS PUBLISHED *Go Set a Watchman* by Harper Lee, the author of *To Kill a Mockingbird*. Some people believed the book had been published against Lee's wishes. Others questioned whether it had been written by Lee at all. Sadly, Lee herself could provide no insight into the matter. She'd had a stroke in 2007 and suffered from dementia until her death in 2016.

Reading *Watchman* depressed me—not only because, in my opinion, it was terrible. But because it had glimmers of brilliance, the promise of a more honest, complex, and devastating portrait of Lee's own father than Atticus Finch had been—a man who struggled with the racial issues of his time, but more often than not clung to the old traditions rather than standing up for change.

I thought a lot about that book, which Lee wasn't able to get right, and about *To Kill a Mockingbird*, which she got *so* right that it catapulted her into the kind of fame and fortune that most writers can only dream of—and stopped her in her tracks.

People sometimes say, "Harper Lee had one book in her, and what a book!"

I don't believe that.

Not long after the publication of *To Kill a Mockingbird*, Lee told a class at Sweet Briar College, "To be a serious writer requires discipline that is iron fisted. It's sitting down and doing it whether you think you have it in you or not. Everyday. Alone. Without interruption. Contrary to what most people think, there is no glamour to writing. In fact, it's heartbreak most of the time."

She also talked about the novels she hoped to write—books that would "leave some record of the kind of life that existed in a very small world…to chronicle something that seems to be very quickly going down the drain. This is small-town middle-class southern life as opposed to the Gothic, as opposed to *Tobacco Road*, as opposed to plantation life." In other words, she said, "all I want to be is the Jane Austen of south Alabama."

The sad thing is, she might have been.

In the 1960s, even a writer who was merely promising rather than established—one whose first novel had received excellent reviews but sold only moderately well—would have been nurtured by her publisher. If she needed money to pay the rent so she could get that second novel written, money magically appeared. The writer's editor would be on call in case of any crisis of confidence, instantly available for lunch or dinner or a drink to help calm the writer down. "Of course, you'll finish the book you're working on," the editor would say. "Of course, it will be wonderful"—and truly mean it. The editor would believe it was her job to guide that writer through the long, harrowing process of birthing the novel inside her.

Harper Lee had all that and more. She had an editor who believed passionately in her work and guided her through revision after revision of both her books. She had friends who believed in her so much that they gave her enough money to quit her job and do nothing but write for a year. But besides *To Kill a Mockingbird*, published in 1960, and *Go Set a Watchman*, released 55 years later, she never finished another book.

In his 2016 biography of Lee, *Mockingbird: A Portrait of Harper Lee, from Scout to Go Set a Watchman*, Charles J. Shields recounts a story about Lee at a party in New York in 2005. A waiter at the party recognized her and, after they'd chatted awhile, asked, "Why didn't you write another book?"

"I had every intention of writing many novels," she reportedly replied. "I never could have imagined the success *To Kill a Mockingbird* would enjoy. I became overwhelmed."

2.

CHERI REYNOLDS WAS THE AUTHOR OF TWO critically acclaimed novels when she mailed off *A Gracious Plenty*—the third of a three-book contract—to her publisher. In return, she received a severance letter. Her editor didn't like the new book enough to take a risk on it since the sales of her first two novels—now out of print and headed for the remainders table—were less than they'd hoped for.

Around the same time, Reynolds lost her teaching job due to a budget crunch.

"It was a real hard season for me," she said. "I was in a mess, holding off bankruptcy a month at a time. I had foolishly been living off of my credit cards, expecting that advance check. It made it seem like maybe I was on the wrong path. I thought maybe my writing was not supposed to be for anyone but me."

Eight months later, Reynolds got a call from Oprah Winfrey, who said she'd chosen *The Rapture of Canaan*, one of those out-of-print novels, as the next Oprah Book Club pick. Within weeks, Reynolds' publisher printed and shipped more than 900,000 copies. They also bid six figures for the book they'd just rejected—a book for which Reynolds had expected no more than $30,000. The university that had let her go miraculously found the funds to rehire her.

Reynolds declined both offers. Instead, she accepted a six-figure offer for *A Gracious Plenty* from a different publisher and signed a contract with a better university.

The Rapture of Canaan sold enough of those 900,000 copies to wipe out Reynolds' financial problems and set her up for years to come. However, the sales of *A Gracious Plenty*—published the following year—were similar to the sales of her earlier books. Reynolds found herself, as a writer, more or less back at square one.

Fame turned out to be a mixed blessing for Cheri Reynolds—though in a different way than the fame that dogged Harper Lee throughout her life. When the Oprah hoopla settled down, Reynolds observed: "I learned [publishing is] not really about the quality of your work. The quality of [my] writing didn't improve just because Oprah picked it, and my value as a writer didn't change either. I might have more readers and more money, but I was the same person who'd been in trouble just months before, with no money and no readers, and no publisher, either. It was a wonderful boost to my career, and an opportunity that I don't expect I'll ever have again. But I knew then, as I know now, that I still had my work to do. My work is not to be a bestselling author. My work is to tell the stories that need to be told."

3.

PERHAPS IT IS A WEIRD BLESSING TO *not* be famous. To not have people anxiously awaiting your next book, ready to judge whether it is better or worse than the one before. To keep the carrot of recognition ever before you—the belief that maybe, just maybe, the novel you're working on right now will be your "breakout" novel.

When it's not, well, you go at it again.

Maybe next time.

Near the end of *Lake Woebegone Days*, Garrison Keillor wrote, "Some luck lies in not getting what you thought you wanted but getting what you have, which once you have got it, you may be smart enough to see is what you would have wanted had you known."

This is exactly the way I feel about my writing life.

I write from my heart, for myself—the only way I know how to write—because it helps me understand myself and the world I live in. And I write because living just one life seems…insufficient. Writing, I can play out my own life differently. I can create whole new lives to live. Imagining the inside of my head, I see a circle of doors, each with the world of one of my novels behind it—except for the one leading to a kind of green room where an assortment of characters wait for me to tell their stories.

The world of my ten-year-old self, setting out to become an author, wasn't wide or rich enough for me to imagine all my life could become. If I could travel backward through time and talk to that girl from where I am now, I'd say:

You will do what you are meant to do, write, but you will be astonished by the strange journey writing will turn out to be. You won't get what you thought you wanted, and that disappointment will shadow you all your life—undermining your confidence, causing you to second-guess decisions you made along the way, making you feel low.

But you'll keep writing because you are a writer and that's what writers do. Sometimes you'll wonder, What if? But then you will remind yourself that no other path would have brought you to this moment in your life, made you the person you are. So, in the end, despite all that's happened, because of all that's happened, you won't want to change a thing.

ACKNOWLEDGMENTS

I worked on *A Commotion in Your Heart* on and off for years, never quite figuring out what it wanted to be—and I'm pretty sure the book wouldn't be in your hands today without the critique, encouragement, discipline, and genius of my writing group. Thank you, Candace Denning, Alison Jester, and Susan Neville.

Thanks to the writers and friends read and commented on the manuscript along the way, including Joan Corwin, Barbara Davis, Margaret-Love Denman, Melissa Fraterrigo, Kathy Higgs-Coulthard, Betsy Childers Lewis, Melody Mansfield, and SJ Rozan.

Thank you to my daughter Kate Shoup for copyediting the manuscript.

To Andrea Boucher for the gift of the book's beautiful design.

To Jim Powell, who founded the Indiana Writers Center, which was there when I finally gathered the courage to write and whose community of writers continues to sustain my writing life.

To the Ragdale Foundation, for the time and solitude I needed to finish the first draft.

And, as always, to my family—Steve, Jenny, Kate, Jim, Olivier, Heidi, and Jake.

www.ingramcontent.com/pod-product-compliance
Lightning Source LLC
Chambersburg PA
CBHW051650040426
42446CB00009B/1075